Self-Publishing
the
Write Way

Ron Fowler

Front Cover Picture: Author Ron Fowler humorously displays his first two successfully self-published books that sold out a total of five printings.

Book Design by Kathy Campbell

This book is not intended as a substitute for legal, accounting or other professional services. If expert assistance is required, the services of a competent professional should be sought.

Dedication

To my good lookin' wife, Kit,
in her role of literary angel's advocate to me.

To my printer, Kurt Gorham,
who makes *me* look good.

To my editor, Mary Ryan,
who puts my commas where they belong.

To all my readers who keep buying this stuff I write.

Introduction

At any given literary moment there must be thousands, perhaps millions, of people around the globe, writing or wanting to write a book. Of those masses, considerably less than one-percent will ever see their work in print. Only a minuscule number of talented writers will ever sell to a major publisher, disappointing odds not unlike winning a lottery.

So where do we go with our cherished manuscripts? Writing two books in two years, more than a hundred publishers/agents, in effect, told me where I could go with mine. Displaying more gutsiness than gray matter, I self-published both. The first, a toe-in-the-water test, sold out profitless that year. The second, selling out four printings totalling over 5,000 books, grossed more than $30,000, aside from expenses. Luck? Somewhat. Skill? Limited. Interesting non-fiction? Very definitely. Marketing ingenuity? Yes, and heaps of hard work.

It would be fascinating to know how many potentially profitable manuscripts are discarded, thrown into the recycle bin, becoming hidden diamonds in the rough that could have produced dividends for their authors.

My *Self-Publishing The Write Way*, written in a lighter vein, describes the various experiences weathered through a couple years of self-publishing. Between these covers I hope you will find it somewhat edifying if you are a "wannabe" author—or perhaps just a bit humorously entertaining if you are anything else.

Already, more than a dozen queried publishers have replied with sorry-slips regarding this book. Perhaps my common sense is as deficient as my writing skills. Think about it. What publisher would buy a manuscript that encourages self-publishing?

Maybe they're telling me to sharpen my axe on someone else's grindstone.

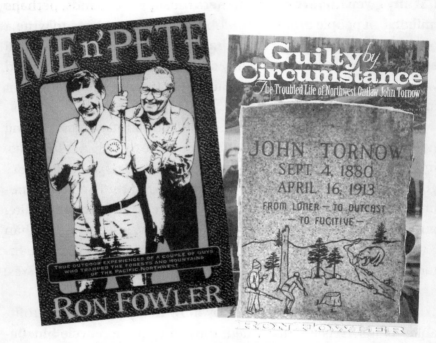

These are the book covers on the author's self-published books, both of which sold out. The popular John Tornow book, based on the life of the Northwest outlaw, sold out four printings, over 5,000 copies.

Prologue

Dusty gravel on the tranquil country lane crunched beneath my Jeep's over-burdened tires on that radiant summer afternoon. The books weighed almost half-a-ton.

The fourth printing of my second self-published book, *Guilty By Circumstance*, the troubled life of Northwest outlaw, John Tornow, just came off the press.

"Careful with that thousand," Kurt, my printer friend had chided me in his farm-country printing shop. "The ink's not dry yet," he joked.

Who could envision that achievement? Book number five thousand reposed somewhere within the twenty white and shiny boxes we'd just loaded.

Retiring after 37-years in the wholesale grocery business, I could answer almost any question which a person could raise about food-things and often did as a volunteer member of "International Executive Service Corps." My wife and I had traveled to Mexico and Russia helping individuals in third world nations establish a wholesale grocery business of their own. But when it came to writing and publishing, I was a neophyte! I'm usually smart enough to know how dumb I am about a lot of things. I had a general idea that writing the story required the application of my pants to the seat of a chair, my fingers on the keyboard in front of me, and words flowing from noggin to paper. Then what? I had no idea. But, I learned!

Writing and then paying to print my own work taught me a multitude of idiosyncrasies about publishing and marketing. I also found that refusing to accept failure in any endeavor requires increased effort be applied to overcome educational voids and valleys.

I look upon quality writing as just one more accomplishment, one that I consistently pursue. I tell myself it's been enough for me to have completed a winning career in other endeavors, really more than enough, but success begets success.

Having scaled one height, other challenges, tougher challenges, beckon. I sense a lump of literary clay on my plate imploring me to transform it into a recognizable winner among written works. Not masterpieces or best-sellers, although that would be all right, just interesting and enjoyable writings that readers would find difficult to put aside.

But, why? What's the point of it all? The reason for writing? Certainly not for monetary rewards, not trying to make lots of money. Most authors recognize burger-flipping pays better. Then is it an ego trip, trying to pull my self-esteem up by my own bootstraps? Consciously, I refute that assertion. But, how well are we attuned to our inner-selves, to our deeply protected psyche? Perhaps unknowingly I write for the anticipated accolades, food for my soul, the pleasure derived from complimentary reader comments, be they puffery or sincere. Attempting to differentiate, I become suspicious. A suspicion that my limited talents could not possibly produce writings worthy of public praise, or even acceptance.

So I continue writing, pursuing an uncertain goal for uncertain rewards. If it produces dollars, that's commendable, but people-praise might constitute a richer remuneration in the form of ego salve. Receiving neither will not become depressing, will not because I must continue writing, if for nothing more than writing in itself.

Heading for home, my literary load reduced the Cherokee's acceleration down the freeway on-ramp as we squeezed in behind a Seattle-bound freighter doing seventy in a sixty zone.

Driving by rote, my concentration was centered not on passing the truck, but on the gnawing need to identify my next writing venture. With two successes in self-publishing why not tackle book number three to make sure the wins were not just "luck?"

In 1996, after national publishers had turned thumbs down on my first manuscript, I self-published it. The book soon sold out, helped by a few friends of *Me N' Pete* in the retail grocery business. Friends like Chuck and Mark Swanson, Chris Pickering, and others lured by the story and locale. The book satisfied a moral obligation to Pete, a witty, happy-go-lucky outdoor friend, who died in 1990. Once printed, the reading public gobbled it up like a featured item in Thursday's grocery ad. Well, my losing two bucks a book did make it a bargain for the buyer, but that initial literary experience taught me a few vagaries about self-publishing.

Back in 1996 our checking account soon reflected a significant dictum. It wasn't a viable business practice to pay the printer $7.00 for a book to sell at wholesale for $5.00. Even in Pete's unbusiness-like habits, he would have known better. His favorite adage had been, "I hope at least to break even on this deal because I sure could use the money."

Who could believe the success of the second book, the true life of Northwest outlaw, John Tornow? In August, 1997, placing the order for the initial printing, my comment to Kurt, "Hope you'll give me a refund on any of these two-thousand that don't sell." Just thinking about all those books made me jittery as a jar of marbles during an earthquake. He smiled, "You'll be back for a second printing."

How did he know? The first batch of books sold out by December, second printing evaporated by March. My bankruptcy concerns diminished when I ordered the fourth press-run in June.

Reality returned while passing the truck, now slowed by the intimidating appearance of a law and order highway patrolman. Smiling at the return to legal truck speeds, thoughts about the numerous ups and downs of self-publishing flitted through my mind like a bevy of butterflies.

The writing experiences provided valuable insight, although not always comprehensible: Like the works of Timothy Leary, some discoveries just boggled my mind. Example, I found that a distributor in Basin, Wyoming held the key to book placement at outlets of a large chain bookseller in Western Washington. This situation seemed a bit flippy.

You can bet your first edition hardcover we soon learned where, when and how to sell books; retail, wholesale, mail-order, mass market, friends, and neighbors.

Cherokee flinched at the piercing shriek of the patrolman's siren as he pulled the big rig over to the highway shoulder. He'd tired of the cat-and-mouse contest.

The pulsating red and blue lights illuminated my thought chamber like a laser light show.

"That's it!" I shouted to nobody except Cherokee. My next book would be a book about writing and publishing books. I would share ideas that worked, or didn't; from experience, a "how-to" of self-publishing; the humorous escapades by a not-so-talented author overcoming mediocrity through "damned if it won't work" determination. At this very moment you're holding book number three, modified to fit your receptive hands.

Chapter 1

Before WWII, rationing, zoot suits, and the Tucker Torpedo automobile, my family lived near the orange groves of southern California. Imagine the thrill for this seven year-old to hit big-time publishing in the local Belvedere Gardens Press. My poem, with the blase, timeworn title, "Bluebirds," sat enshrined at the bottom of column seven, page twenty-three. Wow! The sky was the limit from that day forward. The closing line, "...I often wonder why oh why, we humans cannot also fly." A true masterpiece!

From an early age, writing was the singular outside interest I'd demonstrated aside from normal adolescent pursuits of deviltry and minor mayhem. Mother recalled this proclivity towards literary endeavors as opposed to interests in the manly sciences involving numbers and their combinations.

"He was a poet, not a mathematical child," she once said. "When he was four years-old, sandy-colored curls askew and a wide, triumphant grin, he'd hold up four fingers and proudly announce, "I'm free years old."

As a youngster poetry came easy, so easy in fact that I dashed off several a day. At first my parents encouraged my poetic productivity, but thus motivated, my rhyming creations knew no bounds. I can now imagine that my papering the kitchen walls with a melange of verse probably drove Mom and Dad up those same walls.

At the tender age of eight, I can remember hearing people describe poetry as, "sissy-stuff." Oh, oh, time to graduate to the next literary level. Short stories seemed like a natural. I allowed my imagination to run rampant as I conjured up fictional story lines and breathed life into imaginary characters. We only had radio in those archaic days, no television or "R" rated movies to corrupt our thoughts. Tom Mix and Hopalong Cassidy rode the range of our juvenile imaginations.

Pearl Harbor found our family uprooted to Montesano, Washington, located near the coast. Adults worried about a potential invasion and hoped an ocean would shield us from the enemy. My pals and I just worried about scrounging up a quarter for admission to Saturday's movie matinee.

My next notable break in the publishing business came at the august age of fifteen. Unlike the astounding success she had engineered for me in the poetry arena, Mom now feared my idle hands could lead me to become a ne'er do-well child. Most males can remember how much fun fills their pockets as high school freshmen. There's girls, sports, hangin' out with buds, dates (with girls), assembly hall, skipping class, co-ed dances (with girls). If only life could always be such an adolescent symphony of ongoing merriment.

The collapse of my rollicking good time world came soon after my folks opened the "Playhouse Tavern," a suds-sloshing beer-joint in Montesano that turned into an overnight sellout. Mom became a barmaid. Dad assumed the role of vice-president/ general manager, and on Saturday nights doubled as bouncer. On Sunday morning the prodigal son sorted the empties and swamped out the joint. Just your typical small-town family running a typical small-town business. Dad said the janitorial duties would be "character-building" for me.

The Sunday cleanup chore became an acceptable inconvenience.

It allowed Sunday afternoon for pursuit of....the good times. During this near-puritanical era, alcohol-serving watering holes in

Washington State were closed by law on Sunday. Being head cus-todian at the Playhouse provided me with the key to the firm's one gambling diversion—an ancient, nickel-gobbling one-arm bandit. With this arrangement, who could ever lose? Playing non-stop, whenever the coins were depleted, the machine's cash box do-nated more. This might have been the very first win/win situation for me, but, never did this neophyte gambler leave the premises with any company-owned nickels. The vice-president, charitable as a pre-nup, frowned on my gambling becoming profitable at the tavern's expense.

What does all this folderol have to do with the publishing busi-ness? Be patient, soon you'll understand. It's quite probable Mother and Father worried that I was enjoying life a bit too much, not planning for my future.

"A half-days work once a week, then just five days of school," Mom reminded Pop. "He needs more responsibility."

Drat the luck. My own mother turned against me.

The Playhouse soon established a solid reputation for cold beer, good cheer, and a bartender, (my old man) with a receptive ear.

During the mid-1940's, almost anyone who lived in Montesano and tippled an occasional brew frequented the Playhouse. It would also be a safe assumption nobody in town tippled more beer than "K. C.," the editor of our weekly Montesano *Vidette* Newspaper. (Vidette definition: an outpost in advance of the main army.) Perhaps more than any other customer, "K.C." contributed much to the success of our family business.

Hard-drinking, chain-smoking, ruddy complexioned, his girth at belt-buckle height provided a formidable challenge for our local tailor. Here began the diabolical conspiracy. To say Mom and Dad didn't cater to good ol' "K.C." would be like saying it doesn't rain in Washington's rain forest. They knew which side their beer was bar-reled on.

One fine day my turncoat mother asked the editor, "Do you

have any openings at the paper suitable for our son?"

That question sealed my fate and cast the die in Linotype lead.

Shoving his glass across the bar for the umpteenth refill, the newspaper mogul replied in a slurred voice, "Sure, send him down. We can use him after school and Saturday mornings."

And so began my career as a newspaperman. I became everybody's "gofer." Ted Fosdick, our back-shop honcho, who had a heart big as Colorado, and a sense of humor to match, printed a batch of business cards for me. They were almost too small to hold all the titles he bestowed: Proof-reader; Reporter; Sports Editor; Classified Sales; Advertising; Circulation Director; Office Clerk; Assistant Manager and Janitor; plus a whole bunch of little et ceteras. It soon became quite clear—the newest flunky on the job certainly wore many menial hats on a weekly newspaper.

Pot-bellied "K.C." was a frugal boss. He paid me a meager salary, augmented by perks sure to win the devotion of any teenager.

First, the car. Our rotund editor owned a 1942 Oldsmobile, one of the last built before WWII; club coupe, white, with Hydramatic gearshift. I'd never seen anything so elegant. In our small town that posh vehicle was rare as a vacant cab on the streets of New York City.

On publication day, every Thursday, I was responsible for loading all the mail newspapers into the editor's exquisite Oldsmobile for the short trip to the Post Office which was only one-and-a-half blocks away (nothing was very far away in Montesano). But, in 1944, no teenage boy driving a '42 snow-white Olds took the direct route. A'la James Dean, radio on full blast, arm rested casually on the rolled-down window, sun glasses in place (even on a wet, rainy day), the trunkful of newspapers were driven around town until everyone had recognized the cool driver.

Without a doubt, the boss knew about my extra mileage to the Post Office. Once, the zigzag excursion even included a side-trip to my girl friend's house, four miles away, to show-off the impressive Oldsmobile with me at the wheel. If nothing else, the gas gauge and speedometer would indicate hanky-panky, but "K.C." never batted an eye.

Secondly, while the paycheck was small, the by-lines were unlimited. Everything I wrote was given a "By, Ron" header, so much in fact, Ted Fosdick began addressing me as "Byron."

"One of these days you'll get a by-line on the obituaries," he joked.

My job at the *Vidette* provided a meaningful literary education and taught self-discipline and business acumen. But, good ol' "K. C." imparted limited journalism techniques.

"Don't ever mention snakes or spiders in anything you write," he said, "people dislike crawly things and hate to read about them."

Another favorite teaching was, "Buses you ride on is spelled with one 's.' A kiss (buss) is spelled with two."

Webster approves either spelling. It's uncertain how much proper English was used at the newspaper. Our less-than-educated assistant-editor's oft-asked question around lunch-time was, "Have you et yet?" Good help was hard to find during the war.

At the newspaper in the mid-40's, I learned all about printing and publishing, albeit somewhat antiquated compared with today's methods and machinery. We printed the paper on a humongous flat-bed press almost as long as a school bus.

Two metal-jointed arms pulled the flat newsprint off the huge drum, depositing each printed sheet into a neat stack. Only problem, the arms included a long, perforated gas pipe intended to eliminate static electricity, that emitted a series of tiny blue flames under each sheet of newsprint. Often the press would stop with the flames directly under the paper. POOF!

We usually emptied two fire extinguishers every publication day. "Tiny" McNelly was our pressman, and fortunately, the captain of the volunteer fire department.

Prior to the Japanese surrender of WWII, "K.C." excelled at his pre-planning. We had an entire newspaper printed ahead of time, mostly last week's edition, but including a few updated news articles. The flat sheets (those that hadn't burned) were not dated and the front page had a 3 column x 10-inch blank box in the middle. With lots of advance time, we'd made a separate press run of red ink, splashing an eye-catching, "EXTRA" in three-inch letters across the front page.

When news that the Japanese would surrender came, on Tuesday, August 14, 1945, we only had to workup the, "War Ends," details, print them in the blank box and we were on the street within two hours. Under the, "VICTORY," banner there was the usual "By Ron" article, "Many vacationers enjoy life in Montesano this year."

The *Vidette* job, my first along with mowing Mrs. Hanrahan's lawn every Friday afternoon and the tavern tasks, taught me the old-fashioned way—I earned my money. Ah yes, Mrs. Hanrahan. She was an honest-to-goodness, kick-in-the-pants, little, old, Irish neighbor lady across the street. An impish grin crinkling her lips, Irish eyes twinkling like diamonds set in shamrocks, she'd admonish me, "Now Ronnie, don't ye go at it like ye was killin' snakes."

With such a prestigious job as writing for the *Vidette* and seeing my name in print every week, it was a natural evolution to become editor of our high school newspaper. However, Journalism teacher, Miss McNeill, was a tougher taskmaster than "K.C." Prim and proper, she was a font of knowledge and skill, patiently teaching us raw recruits the basic writing techniques. The mission statement of our weekly, *Montesano Bulldog*, proclaimed, "For better coverage of high school news and gossip." Such a lofty goal.

Upon my graduation, the *Vidette* offered me full-time employment, but, it seemed logical to move along to bigger literary opportunities. In the nearby town of Hoquiam, the Washingtonian, a morning daily newspaper, needed a sports editor.

I soon learned that a small daily paper differed little from a small weekly. In addition to the sports desk, city news was also an assigned responsibility. So once again the obituaries fell into my reluctant literary hands.

After working a few months, I found the publication was struggling. A hurry-up reality check indicated it would be expeditious for me to struggle out of there. Unrelated to my resignation, the paper folded a short time later.

In 1948, for the very first time, self-publishing landed square amid-ship my career journey. Together with a fellow high school graduate who had also been my good friend and editor of our school yearbook, I formed a partnership to publish a monthly outdoor magazine. The *Harbor Sportsman* covered the Olympic Peninsula of Western Washington State. We had two employees—he and I.

Paul and I rented all we could afford, a slum-lord delight in a seedy part of town. As if joined at the hip, we functioned as one. We lived, ate, worked, wrote, even went out on dates together. Our girl friends were also friends.

Paul insisted he knew how to cook so those responsibilities fell into his domain. Short on finances, we squeezed every dime, even more so on groceries. Julia Child would never have approved the culinary catastrophes developed on our grease-spattered cookstove. If there had been a charitable soup kitchen in town, we would have been their best customers.

During springtime, a small river-running fish called smelt migrate into streams of Western Washington. Fishermen catch them by the ton, so retail prices for the silvery hordes are as low as sea-level.

Paul's favorite bill of fare became fried smelt and sliced parsnips, well-blackened. Watching him prepare our meal one day, I wondered why he dumped the smelt into the frying pan just as they came from the fish market.

"Shouldn't they be cleaned and the heads removed?" I asked

my associate publisher, now chief cook.

Shooting me a look that would turn away sharks, he replied, "No, I always fry them like this. They're not big enough to have any innards that will hurt us." On that point we differed.

I've never been very thrilled about eating smelt, even when they have been properly eviscerated. These weren't. Cooking controversies began to come between us.

We both interviewed and wrote our own outdoor articles, did all photography, sold ads and subscriptions, prepared copy for the printer, and distributed the magazine each month.

We were surprised when the first month's edition, 28-pages, color cover, 300 copies, broke even, including rent and vittles.

Operationally it went smoother than Grandma's mashed potatoes at Thanksgiving dinner.

In a very short time, too much togetherness and uncleaned smelt took their toll. Our working relationship became as sticky as an overcooked fondue pot. Paul bought out the partnership while I hit the unemployment line.

Working alone, my former partner published several bigger and better editions of the magazine, but soon folded due to his inability to collect for ads and subscriptions. We often ponder what successes might have been ours if we'd developed our partnership and continued publication. The magazine was an instant winner with outdoor people in Western Washington.

Upon dissolution of the partnership, (which consisted of packing up my typewriter, clothes and blankets, a few chipped dishes, two pencils and a dull pair of scissors), my writing was put aside in favor of a new job with a wholesale grocery company. Sometimes a first love must be forsaken in a realistic decision to pursue more viable, income-producing opportunities.

The changes in careers soon confirmed the food business put more pork and beans on the table than did publishing magazines. Especially outdoor magazines with a 24-hour-a-day-partner who wasn't fussy about frying smelt. In one paragraph, my grocery career spanned 37-years with the same company, from warehouseman to Executive Vice-President, to retirement at 55 in 1985. I'd been in the right place, at the right time, accepted responsibilities, welcomed advancements and change, and was not afraid of hard work. I was also extremely lucky.

Still, it was difficult to turn a chosen business pursuit into an avocation. Even after marriage, freelance writing and photography occupied spare time hours not devoted to the grocery business.

To accommodate my photo hobby, an unfinished bedroom at home was transformed into a darkroom. A common bathroom wall provided easy access for water and drains. For the 1960's era, my equipment—cameras and enlarger—were quite downtown. A local dealer persuaded me to buy a used Hasselblad camera—the epitome of picture-taking—ten dollars down, ten dollars a month for the remainder of my life. The only problem, the Hasselblad knew a heck of a lot more about photography than I did.

With monthly payments, it now became necessary to generate more freelance income. Often it was past midnight when I went to bed, then up at five-thirty the next morning for a regular shift stacking groceries at the wholesaler's warehouse.

In addition, I found it mentally rewarding to teach a group of 4-H kids photography. My son, Dave, joined the sessions, meeting in our improvised darkroom. With all the extracurricular activities, it seemed my candle burned at all *three* ends.

Photography became a full-time hobby, shooting news and feature photos for various publications. I decided to freelance only in photography, avoiding the time-consuming writing, except photo captions. Soon it became depressingly obvious that pictures alone wouldn't make me rich and famous. Especially rich. Spending a couple of hours on a shoot, rushing to my homemade darkroom for a couple more hours, beating a path to the local city editor's desk with my finished, b & w, 8 X 10's, netted me a sale of three dollars. With exceptional photos, sometimes he'd buy two— six dollars.

Complaining to the editor about my poverty level photo income, he queried, "Why don't you start writing feature articles to accompany your pics? Then we could pay more for your work."

So I went back to my typewriter while the photos were washing in the darkroom. My hobby income skyrocketed to eight or ten dollars for five or six hours work. I wrote about and photographed everything from a farmer's amazing long-hair goat with 18-inch spiral horns; to a barn owl's new litter of owlets perched high atop a smelly silage silo; to various auto and train accidents around the county.

An increase of feature articles in local newspapers and magazines provided more bylines and reverse notoriety. The publicity was welcomed, but the same spotlight identified the growing amount of extracurricular activity. Although my work at the wholesaler was satisfactory, they became wary of the increased sideline ventures.

One day my boss confronted me, "Ron, is your career path heading into the wholesale grocery business or do you plan a literary profession?"

Thinking back on those three-dollar checks for one picture, and the five hours work involved, required only split-second decision making for me to announce that groceries would be my life-long occupation. My hourly warehouse wage had already reached the lofty figure of three bucks an hour. My folks didn't raise a dummy incapable of making that comparison. Although writing and photography were still my first-loves, they wouldn't pay the mortgage, let alone the orthodontist.

Upon receiving my commitment to groceries, the boss said, "Our management wants to begin grooming someone to take my place when I retire and we think you're the best candidate."

Goodbye journalism, hello management training! It was fun while it lasted.

Akin to the grocery business, I met a dry-humored, Schilling spice salesman, Pete Grimes, during the mid-1950's. Pete and I became good friends, camping, hunting, fishing, hiking in the Northwest outdoors for thirty-five years. Pete grew up on the flat plains of Kansas, entering the world at Salina in 1912, seventeen years my senior. With a glint of humor in his eyes, he once told me, "Growing up, we were so poor, we couldn't even afford cobwebs. All our spiders moved across the street to take up residence with a family that was destitute."

He became the primary subject of my first self-published book, *Me N' Pete*. From the book's Introduction:

> "Pete was a comfortable, fun guy to be with, and like a rambunctious pup, humor romped between us."

Our two common bonds were a deep fondness for the outdoors, and our appreciation of, and ability to communicate humor. When schedules permitted, we spent weekends and vacations pursuing outdoor adventures from moose hunting in British Columbia, steelhead fishing in the Northwest, and hiking mountains on Washington's Olympic Peninsula. Considerably scaled-back, my occasional freelance writing or photo articles resulted from some of these experiences.

Always the comic, Pete became my willing outdoor photographic model for a few humorous photo essays. One gig illustrated clam digging at our ocean beach. We dug a huge hole in the sand, must have taken us half-a-day, had to beat the incoming tide. Only Pete's boots were visible, protruding into the air like a giant clam had pulled him down the hole.

Another article expounded on preparedness when mountain hiking. Roped to a cliff, he carried bicycle, snowshoes, blowtorch, and upside-down map.

Pete's humor knew no bounds. To my invitation, "Let's sneak away from work Wednesday and go fishing," he replied,

"Can't go Wednesday, that's my day off."

Another wry comment of his: "My first job delivering beer in Chicago required a character witness. I told them to phone my brother. He'd verify that I was a character."

"They tell me I've got a big nose. But they seem to forget this is a small room we're in and everything just looks bigger."

Perhaps the happiest day in Pete's life came when he retired from, as he put it, "being a pepper peddler." Planning ahead for the momentous event, he bought a new pickup truck, "..for my 30-foot trailer to push around the country."

By then, I'd moved my family to Salem, Oregon. Pete wrote, "I'll have to admit I had mixed emotions about retirement. Those emotions were; happiness, joy, ecstacy, elation, gaiety, jubilance, and exultation."

Although engrossed at this time with my wholesale management responsibilities, me n' Pete took time to hike and hunt, fish and fracas in our cherished Pacific Northwest outdoors. Each outing provided typewriter fodder for future feature articles. Most of the writing and pictures we took were tossed into a drawer, saved but not forgotten. It became my avowed responsibility to put the material together someday in book form, publish, or have it published.

One of my deepest regrets involves not proceeding with the book during Pete's lifetime. Every once in awhile, from overhead, it seems I can hear his haunting wisecrack, "Well, it's about time you got up off your backside (not Pete's term) and did something for a change. Jeez, do I hafta do everything around here?"

Content with an unrealistic belief in immortality—just never giving death a second thought—Pete's demise in 1990 smacked my conscious being like a planet-size meteor. It couldn't happen—we would go on forever—but this solid friendship came to a sad and sudden conclusion.

Lulled into a sense of evermore, my procrastination about the book laid a heavy guilt trip on my conscience. But the feeling of remorse fueled the burning determination within me to eventually dedicate the necessary time to research, plan and write the book about our fun times together.

Chapter 2

"Start writing!" My subconscious elfin muse repeated annoyingly as I sat at my desk, freshly sharpened pencil clutched in benumbed fingers. My mind was blank as a pauper's last will and testament.

Where to start? This first book-writing foray appeared more complex than the simple assignments of banging out short stories. Again came the prodding of my subliminal goblin, "You can eat an elephant by taking one bite at a time." The little twit became relentlessly obnoxious—infallible but obnoxious.

There seemed to be an immense fear tugging at my psyche, an insurmountable obstacle preventing me from charging out of the literary starting blocks. It couldn't be a fear of failing, that was an unknown deterrent to me. Always aiming high, striving for perfection, I'd chased the rewards of success throughout my lifetime, seldom experiencing a major tumble. But undeniably, my writing skills were as out of shape as an overweight body on a health spa treadmill.

Through it all my solemn pledge to write the book to Pete's memory became the engine that drove me forward. My library card provided the key to higher learning as I read several, "How to's" pertaining to book authorship. Now I felt better.

I learned the most important first step in writing anything of value is to develop a road map. If Azusa is the goal it's easy to get stuck in Anaheim without a dependable Rand-McNally.

Planning, detailing, organizing the material, step-by-step getting from introduction to foreword to Chapter One through Chapter Forty 'leven is almighty important. Lay out the basics, not the final groomed sentences; those will come later as cherished passages are upgraded and rewritten, probably several times, gaining specificity from each adjustment.

The books tell us, "Write it rough, write it out of focus, write it wrong, but above all write, write, write."

I rewrote *Pete* (thus titled here for succinctness) three times, but fortunately only threw it away twice. I soon learned each rewrite pushed the manuscript a notch higher on the improved reading scale. From ground zero, my potential upper-level betterment plateaus were abundant. Reviewing the final self-published book today, I can spot portions that might benefit from tighter scrutiny. Experience is a progressive teacher. Hindsight always rates A-plus on the report card of our reviews.

Lack of brevity is an Achilles' heel in my writing endeavors. But that's only one of many. To itemize all shortcomings would require the multiple heels of a centipede. Constant review of rough drafts highlight unnecessary verbiage, like the word "constant" in this sentence. Just when I've cut to the bone, my wife Kit reviews one of the written pages, slashing off six more redundancies and a couple of windy sentences with her thunderbolt eraser. Her normal wide-open brown eyes narrow to the thin slits of a heartless executioner as she attacks my wordy prose. Following this orgy of eliminating verbosity, her countenance of innocence returns, "There, that will be so much better." What would I ever do without this woman?

I began my research and collecting facts following Pete's death in 1990. The review of his files, notes, letters and financial affairs landed on my narrow and bony shoulders. Previously he had appointed me as executor with the comment, "I'll probably still be around to dance at your funeral, but just in case...."

Always the comic, he left many notes directed to me knowing

one day I'd be sifting through his papers to determine what needed to be done. On a used envelope Pete had scrawled, "Nothing important in this envelope but I know you'll look anyway because you never believe me." In his "personal" file I discovered a note in his unique, scribbly writing: "Give that antique freezer out in the garage to Stan. It's older than he is and almost as useless but he's always wanted it." Recognition like this from Pete was a compliment.

Another reminder written on a Winston carton-back: "Don't forget you still owe me $10,000 from that last bet. I plan to collect." We often made preposterous wagers, both recognizing the other would never pay up.

At the bottom of the document-pile was one more dictate aimed at me. "Why are you still spending time going through all this junk? Go fishing, have a drink or something. Enjoy yourself or you'll sooner than later be down here with me." Pete was a strong advocate of the, "have fun today, maybe work tomorrow" philosophy. I always aimed my after-death comments to him, "up there," but here he'd predicted himself being down south.

I gleaned considerable typewriter fodder from Pete's files, some of which I would not have received when he was alive, he believing it unworthy. Nevertheless, I'd recommend live interviews from prospective book characters (Pete certainly was that) rather than postmortems.

Another source of material for my initial manuscript came from my complete collection of *Now* magazines, a periodical printed monthly by my employing wholesale grocery company. During my first year of employment working in the warehouse I unsuccessfully applied for the vacated position of editor of this informative and well-read publication. Before I retired, the editor position reported to me.

In years past I contributed zany stories to the company slick about outdoor escapades by me n' Pete. Misadventures such as,

"Don't Go With Harvey," a trouble-ridden experience we endured on horseback with an unfit Idaho outfitter. "Due north to Cedar Creek," described an ocean beach hike through the pristine sands of Washington's Olympic National Park.

"Showdown with Mama," told of a harrowing experience with a mother black bear who misinterpreted our intentions with her burly cub.

The *Now* magazine articles provided the basis for several chapters in the *Pete* book. In lieu of having published short stories, "wannabe" book authors could benefit from writing about experiences, then saving them for future reference. Without memory jogging stories or voluminous notes, aging gray matter can forget even recent happenings. Besides, the writing practice helps build character and energizes brain cells.

In flipping through the 1,361 pages of my *Rodale Synonym Finder*, I'm reminded it is as important to my writing as a steering wheel is to a car. Without either, we couldn't arrive at a destination. Someone suggested this fabulous writing aid early on, and I refer to it at every paragraph. This thesaurus contains over one million synonyms, a decided advantage over the paltry 45,000 on my word processor. (My first weary *Rodale*, pages ripped and missing, went to its happy hunting ground. I'm now on my second.) They're inexpensive, any book store.

Another source of material was Kit's daily journal which she's kept almost since she learned to write. Surprisingly she had logged a viable record of our miscreant adventures. I unearthed entries such as: "Well, the two playboys are off on another day-long fishing trip to Lord only knows where, or cares. Guess I'd better hustle off to the fish market if we're going to have seafood for dinner."

One sarcastic abbreviated note back in 1987 bemoaned: "Ron bought new hiking boots, old ones got dirty." It was followed a week later: "Hubby's back is paining him, poor thing. Said he strained it while he and Pete hiked the Olympics."

After gathering all the aforementioned material, the next task was to put it into chronological sequence. Let's see now, did we catch all those salmon before we fished steelhead on the Cowlitz River or after. Was it 1968 or '69 that we limited on razor clams at Copalis Beach? A memory enhancement course might have been helpful, but Kit's journal sufficed. I'd procrastinated too long to benefit from Pete's input. Like overcooked oatmeal, my data retention was becoming mushy.

Once the material was sorted and sequenced, the actual writing task confronted me. I had this gargantuan pile of every conceivable type of paper carefully arranged by dates. A gust of wind would have exploded this mass like a pot of Chinese chow-chow. Pray the winds remain becalmed.

Lacking complete confidence in my writing quality, I contacted professional editor/consultants to review my chapters, and suggest improvements or modifications—sort of a reality check. My front office (Kit) reviews the rough drafts of any masterpiece in current production. I value her input because she's adept and a voracious speed-reader, famous throughout our far-flung family for knocking out a whole Tom Clancy novel before bedtime.

My punctuation is atrocious. Shaking her head in disbelief, my wife says, "You put commas where they don't belong and leave them out where they do." I must have been staring out the window during high school English composition classes. Or, like these two commas, I've just forgotten the rules dictating their placement. Calculating the odds, I've begun leaving out most commas recognizing the potential error factor drops to 50-50.

After Kit's review, my critical writing consultant lends immeasurable improvement to my literary stumblings. My wife's consultant fees for her editing are negligible. (My turn to wash the dishes). But the experience factor of the pro's (no prose intended) and knowledge of current literary trends are a decided advantage. You will find that a competent, yet reasonable editor, one not afraid to tell you when you've got your head up your back pocket, is worth their weight in sterling reviews. Outlining chapters, they can assist developing your bookish road map. Might prevent you from getting high-centered.

Some brains must short-circuit when fingers connect to electronic devices. Much to my frustration, I cannot compose meaningful dialogue or sockeroo story lines when tied to a machine. Some will say I can't under any conditions, period. (Does that comma belong there?)

When writing, my cerebral functioning seems to go on strike unless I have a stubby pencil grasped between right thumb and forefinger, eraser on the northern end. Recently I've graduated to a mechanical pencil which seems to be marginally conducive to development of adequate brain waves. Like Shakespeare and Longfellow, we craft our manuscripts the old-fashioned way—we handwrite them. My only redemption, I've talked to others trapped in the same quandary, they say old customs die hard. During my ignominious writing days, I've probably trashed enough lined legal pads to decimate a Crown-Zee woodlot. I favor the yellow paper. Do you suppose they make those yellow ones from lemon trees?

Once thoughts have been manually transferred to paper, I have no problem entering the linguistics into one of man's marvelous machines. Here again I've graduated from manual typewriter to word processor. Perhaps I'm harking back to my caveman days, but the cordless Underwood or Royal uprights were hard to beat. And you literally had to beat the livin' tweedle out of them. Never liked electrics, the touch was never "write" for me. (Kit says this "write" is hokey!) (Comment by ed. 'She's "write".') It stays.

My Brother Processor does a commendable job of mechanically capturing my wordy input, reproducing or storing each profound passage. But I have a tremendous distrust for any machine that is smarter than I. I've never allocated the time necessary to absorb the entire 300-page owner's manual. I know my 5600-MDS is just sitting there smirking at me in my stupefied state of unenlightened bliss.

A myriad of whistles, bells, keys and knurls exist on my word machine that I never use, or know how to. So many that on occasion, when I accidentally jostle the wrong knob, all hell breaks loose. It bellows like an abused banshee and shifts into an uncontrollable meltdown phase. Then I'm forced to research the manual to learn how to return to common-folk functions.

Maintenance? I brushed, cleaned out eraser debris, washed the keys with lighter fluid once a year on my faithful aging Underwood—maybe a new ribbon every other year. Nothing more.

But this new, anemic twentieth-century, electromechanical wonder of mine frequently requires 911 urgency attention at the electronics hospital. A transistor chip here, an internal memory failure there, always something different to go on the fritz.

Thank goodness for extended warranties.

But I must be honest. The computer/word processor certainly provides amenities unknown to Underwood aficionados. An entire book stored on that little three-inch floppy disc? It seems impossible. Move that paragraph from Chapter One to Chapter Two? My Underwood blushes with embarrassment. You're kidding, it'll do that? Certain word processor models check for punctuation errors. But the program is quite limited, at least on my Brother. Checking on the "will do—won't do", I discover it's no help in comma placement. But, I'll have to admit the electronic era is the way to better book beginnings, and my advice is to learn the "ins and outs" of your computer or word processor in order to avoid my follies.

As modern technology hammers down prices of full-scale computers and their capabilities skyrocket, you may wish to consider this more sophisticated type of word processing for your writing ventures. The experts tell us that transferring electronic data to hard copy can follow more varied and efficient avenues from computer disks vs. less sophisticated single-function word processors. I recall that my friendly printer, Kurt Gorham, performed electronic somersaults in converting my word processor disks to his cyber-system, and would have much preferred my using a programmable computer to process book manuscripts. I'd suggest you find out what your printing company prefers, then keep them happy by providing data input compatible with their systems. You could reap bountiful rewards through reduced book printing costs.

Next came the time for the "Quick brown fox to jump over the lazy dog." Pencils and mind sharpened, blank yellow pads stacked like neat cordwood, I resolved to begin writing the first book. How and where? The where was easiest so I tackled it first. I prefer quiet and comfort; fortunately I have both in a tucked away, downstairs corner office that also affords a magnificent view of Washington's Puget Sound. If comfortable settings are important for literary quality, I should have no excuse for not pumping out a best-seller. But not all writers prefer silence and solitude. Some may want the TV blaring; kids running through the rooms terrorizing each other at full lung capacity, punctuated by the neighbor's medley of audacious radio babble at volume setting nine. To each his own decibel.

With the where established, next came the how—a bit more difficult. I prefer to make a general chapter-by-chapter outline, then tackle each chapter more in depth. I scribble out a multitude of simple sentences identifying a thought or a situation, then number each in the appropriate sequence for the chapter. In the *Pete* book, right up front I wanted to provide brief insight to our growing up years, but I also needed a "grabber" which I felt was important for creating interest in each beginning. This is how *Pete* all began:

"Look out! Here it comes," Bobby shouted. Having vowed to stand fast in front of the onrushing iron dragon, we awaited our fate in the warm afternoon sun. Rivulets of perspiration trickled down our smudgy young faces as the steel monster, snorting clouds of black smoke, thundered toward us. A dangerous game, but for us kids the pinch of risk was worth big-time thrills."

Those opening lines launched my first self-published book, *Me N' Pete*, onto an unfamiliar readership in 1996. In a Norman Rockwell setting, the story began when I was twelve years-old and pestering serene neighborhoods with my pals in the small country town of Montesano, Washington during the 1940's. Nothing serious; steal a few apples from Mrs. Carter's orchard, clatter sticks along Fournier's picket fence, chase old man Gleeson's cat up their holly tree. When not terrorizing serene neighborhoods around the village, we played a game called "chicken." This potentially dangerous pursuit required us to stand on the railroad tracks and stare down onrushing steam engines. Our bravado marched ahead of our common sense but woe to the first scaredy-cat who turned away. This dangerous game undoubtedly elevated the veteran locomotive engineer's blood pressure and caused him a Medicare moment, but growing up was such a bore. Thank goodness for the presence of an Almighty Benefactor who enshrouds scatterbrain kids with a protective coating.

I also devoted a page in the opening chapter to Pete's childhood days, then rolled onward with the book's primary theme of the humorous outdoor escapades we hatched in the Pacific Northwest.

As I began writing and the dialogue unfolded, it all seemed right to me—the laughs—the wordplay—the banter we'd exchanged—the outdoor experiences, as vivid then as when they'd happened. From my notes and even more from memory, page after yellow-pad written page literally flew into the "save" basket. Excited with the book's forward progress, and with pardonable pride, I was as "amped up" as though I'd guzzled down a double Starbucks espresso.

Now try to stay with me on this.

After a few pages, I'd shuffle back to the chapter's beginning, review what I'd written. I did this often, never failing to make at least one correction; change a word, delete another. This was an ongoing ritual. Sometimes in haste, trying to finish a chapter, the review process was shortchanged and quality suffered. So I tried to realistically allot the hours necessary to re-read what I'd written. Several times.

I discovered that if manuscript development time was interrupted for a period of days or weeks, it became difficult to begin anew without reading the previous pages, or chapters.

I tried developing short sentence, chapter summaries describing specific incidents or certain dialogue. This I could use to quickly review, chapter-by-chapter, what I'd already applied to paper. This soon became cumbersome. I relied instead on just reviews and re-reads to avoid duplication. Sort of an—"if it ain't broke, don't fix it" mode.

Reviewing the chapters, I felt satisfied with the work up to that point. Without a doubt it would become a best-seller, number one on the top-ten, a Pulitzer no less, later the movie adaptation ...doesn't every author feel that way about their first literary creation?

Thinking back on the writing I've done, it seems quite important that an author be totally familiar with the subject matter. I cannot begin to fathom writing a book, or even a short article, without tons of research or a thorough knowledge of the manuscript's basic theme. That applies to non-fiction with which I am most familiar. On the other hand, fiction writing probably requires an unlimited imagination and organizational technique to put it all together.

One of my caustic reviewers once inquired, "Ron, what is the primary theme of your book?" His brier patch eyebrows jiggled at each word, and his tone reflected his difficult restraint from making critical comments.

Recognizing the obviously loaded question, I managed a thin smile in replying, "*Me N' Pete*, of course."

"Then why in the world are you describing a Mexican bullfight in Chapter Four?" he asked, emitting a sigh of discouragement.

"Sorry, I'll zoom us literally back to trout fishing on a bubbling stream in the Pacific Northwest."

The incident was embarrassing but provided a necessary learning experience. I imagined the reviewer might have thought I'd taken dunce lessons. He probably told his literary compatriots that I was one of the few authors he'd reviewed who wrote a book within a book. What a hoot!

This was somewhat typical of my writing weaknesses that I needed to concentrate on for improvement. I often find myself drifting off the main subject highway onto an obscure side road to nowhere. I believe this occurs when an indefinite chapter outline weakens the subject continuity. Before long, one sentence leads to another, then another unrelated, and soon I'm battling bulls instead of me n' Pete landing rainbow trout up north. Concentration, staying focused on the subject, and a strong chapter outline will help remedy this ailment. Wish I could always remember that.

Seldom do I predetermine the length of my books. I'm certain the pro's will raise their collective eyebrows at this admission. Like the dedicated merchant who just kept selling below cost until the money was all gone, I just keep writing until the paper and pencils are all gone. Well, not really. I usually have a moveable goal in mind. The *Pete* book went overboard on length. But I was having too much fun to quit. Not a very professional approach towards word-sculpting a book. If chapters run away wild with verbiage and get out of hand, it's possible to make *Gone With The Wind* look like a novelette. Transferring rough, yellow-sheet copy to first-draft word processor copy, I soon found I had 480 typed, double-spaced (as editors insist) pages. This would equate to approximately 340-pages in a soft-cover, 6x9 inch book. Whacking out bushels of my verbosity would reduce the book's heftiness like I'd sent it to Weight Watchers. In layman terms (laywoman?), it was a double-wide, a literary porker, but strictly on a pound-by-pound evaluation, a bargain at under ten bucks at the counter.

However, in reality, for economy of scale, the monster needed to weigh-in at no more than 256-pages, text, pictures, ISBN page, commas, et all. And that's where it ended up after I made a few minor cutbacks and Gorham's used a smaller, squeezed-up type face—a bargain read at $9.95. But not very profitable!

Ah yes! Happiness is a thick manuscript, a new toothbrush, and a full tank of gas.

Chapter 3

Although I began researching and collecting input for my *Pete* book in 1990, the serious writing began in 1993-94. I had trashed earlier versions of the manuscript which included Mexican bull-fighting and all that diversionary trivia. Having learned my lessons from Experience #101, taught by meticulous reviewers, at last I felt Pete was headed in the right direction under the tutelage of my editor, Mary Ryan.

With diligence I could crank out a 6,000-word chapter monthly; considerably less when household maintenance projects or pro-longed fishing trips interfered. My newly retained editor moni-tored the rehabbed output, offered constructive modifications, and sent me back to my stubby pencils with renewed enthusiasm. I popped the much improved pages into my Brother gizmo and let the story roll with vivid verbs and graphic adjectives from my newly honed cognitive ability.

Finishing several chapters, I felt it was a propitious time to let the better-known publishing houses begin to outbid each other for the rights to *Pete*. Let's see, I mused, Time-Warner; Simon and Schuster; Little, Brown Company; where should I send it? Which house de-served it?

Undaunted by never having written a literary query letter in my entire life, I naively slammed together a half-page, "Would you like to publish this book?" missive. Next, I selected three of the "big-boys" and fired off query letters with sample chapters. Surprisingly, I knew enough to include a SASE (Stamped, Self-addressed Envelope) for return of the material. Sure, I knew all about this publishing protocol.

I calculated. Three days for my query to arrive at their New York offices. Perhaps two days for it to reach one of their influential editors. If they *really* liked it, I could get a phone call within a week. If they used the mails (after all, they couldn't send me a check over the phone), I should receive their offer within 10-14 days.

I waited—and waited some more. I nitpicked our postal service if our mail delivery was later than 10:00 a.m. It seemed impossible that all three queries could have been lost in the mail. But what other explanation when I'd heard nothing by the end of the first month? Where had I gone wrong?

All of a sudden and all at once a light bulb beamed over my head. As the saying goes, "I got my smarts." Once again I became a frequent visitor to our little hometown library. I researched the book, *Literary Market Place,* (L.M.P.) and "how-to" books on writing a query letter and submitting manuscripts. Among my favorites: *How To Write a Book Proposal*, by Michael Larsen; *Getting Your Book Published*, by Robert W. Bly; *The Sell Your Novel Tool Kit*, by Elizabeth Lyon.

I learned that queries for fiction and non-fiction books can differ in their structure and composition. The plot is usually the focal point of most fiction, so authors are advised to use a query letter outlining the plot to solicit interest from editors/agents. If a letter detailing the plot sparks interest with an editor, there will usually be an invitation to send additional material including sample chapters.

With all this newly acquired knowledge tucked away in my upper-story, I bombarded publishers in a frontal attack. I polished my query letter, expanded on the proposal package, selected names and addresses of large, medium and small-press publishers. I calculated that fifteen queries would have a better chance than three. Over a two-month period, I single-handedly almost wiped out the postal department's national debt. Outbound costs were bad enough, the enclosure of return postage for the bulky proposal packages began to shrink my balance sheet, as well as my ego.

Eight weeks into the book query program, my first publisher reply arrived. Recognizing my own SASE envelope was a real downer. If they were returning my sample chapters, I deduced the publisher wasn't wildly enthusiastic about *Pete*. In the envelope was a standard, printed form; "Sorry, your material does not fit our present format." Such a nice way to put it when you know they really mean, "We have absolutely no interest in this stuff." Even the signature was machine-printed, instead of handwritten.

Always the optimist, I thought, well what the heck! There's about a dozen more queries and proposals floating around out there that haven't called home yet. The reality of the book business became painfully obvious. Maybe this wouldn't be as easy as I'd first thought. However, my writing and querying was as experimental as Orville and Wilbur's.

Each mail brought more, "Thanks, but no thanks," returns. I formulated a new tactic. For every rejection notice, I vowed to send out two new queries/proposals. Quantity supersedes quality. I scurried around, busier than Alice's White Rabbit.

Library visits to scribble new lists of publishers from the in-house L.M.P. reference book became a weekly occurrence. With my ever-increasing expenses, I sure couldn't afford to buy one of those big hummer reference books. Huge postage bills stared me right in the checkbook. I think that was the year postal authorities decided a postage rate increase was unnecessary; probably because I'd pushed them onto the black side of the ledger.

One day a wonderful thing happened. I received my first *hand-written* rejection slip, not printed, it was even hand-signed by the editor. "Your sample chapters are very interesting. Unfortunately we have filled our printing quota for the year. You might want to try us again next year or seek another publisher. Good luck."

I went back to the library's L.M.P. and read that on average that particular publisher printed two books a year. Without the assistance of my calculator, I determined my chances of fattening our bank account with this firm were rather slim.

Rejection slips began arriving like machine gun bullets bouncing off a Tiger tank. I'd heard the horror stories of "wannabe" authors receiving multitudes of "sorry" notices. The cliche of, "receiving sufficient rejection notices to paper a bedroom wall" wasn't really a cliche with me. It was factual. I quit counting at sixty-seven, but the design of the new wall paper was rather charming.

"Don't become discouraged," Kit said. Then she told of one best-selling author who received ninety-four rejections before selling her first book. That was minimally uplifting. I had twenty-seven to go.

Another rejection from a mid-size publisher contained a personally-typed letter from one of the firm's editors: "I rather liked the sample chapters from your *Pete* book. Unfortunately, when I took the material to our editorial board I could not obtain a consensus for consideration." This rekindled my flickering publishing flame as perhaps it was intended to do. However, it left me no recourse, no action I could take to enhance my chances with this publisher. In effect, it was just another rejection notice, a good read but no brass ring.

Since those early days of turndowns, I have read extensively on the proper method of submitting query letters followed by the sophisticated book proposal. A query asking, "Would you like to publish this manuscript?" doesn't seem to cut it.

Depending on which "how-to" book is read, non-fiction book proposals to potential publishers can be six to sixty pages long. Seems like a few short books might almost be exceeded in length by the proposal to "sell" them. There are specific steps for non-fiction book proposals, my area of concentration.

First, I would suggest a brief cover letter. Its main purpose is to thank the editor/agent for their time reviewing your material. Tucked into the letter might be a self-addressed postcard acknowledging receipt of your hernia-size book proposal package that includes sample chapters. The postcard is intended as a receipt for the author mailed back by the receiving editor. It's cheaper than sending the whole enchilada via certified mail, and your frugality is sure to impress the editor/lit agent.

Next, you'll need to float a loan to pay postage on this big hummer *and* the SASE to bring it back; that's the killer. We're told by the American Society of Journalists and Authors: "A proposal is a detailed presentation of the book you want to write. It includes a description of the book, the likely market for it, a chapter by chapter outline, an author's bio, and a sample chapter or two."

This is one suggested format for a non-fiction book proposal as suggested by several of the pro's:

1 TITLE PAGE. A nice, clean, unsoiled sheet of white paper headed, "Book Proposal." Center the title, author's name on the next line. In the lower corner enter your name, address, phone and fax number. (The publisher needs to know where to mail the royalty check.)

2. PROPOSAL CONTENTS. Make a table of contents for your proposal. Be succinct. (If that went over your head, make it short and sweet.)

3. OVERVIEW. In brief form tell the who what, why, when, where and how about your book.

4. TARGETED AUDIENCE. Tell what segment of the reading public will be interested in your book. Why?

5. AUTHOR BIO. Tell the editors about yourself, your credentials for writing the book, other writing you have done.

6. SUGGESTED MARKETING. How would you sell and promote your book? Would you be available to participate in the marketing? Would you fly to New York to accept a "Best Seller" award or to Big Rock, Idaho to sign a book for Mrs. Reightenour at Fleagle's Bookstore?
7. COMPETITION. Are there books in print that would compete with yours? If so, how is yours different?
8. CHAPTER OUTLINE. A one-paragraph summary of each chapter's content, providing a hard-hitting outline intended to "sell" the editor on your book.
9. SAMPLE CHAPTER. Consider enclosing all or portions of a sample chapter so the editor can evaluate your writing skills and knowledge of the subject.

Query letters for works of fiction are usually limited to just one page, written in a few well-chosen words. Often it is more difficult to proficiently compose a single page of concise statements than it is to write a half-dozen rambling pages sure to turn off even the most patient editor.

The novel-query letter is the author's first and only opportunity to elicit (or excite) an editor's interest. The initial paragraph should contain the vitals: Author's name, title, genre, book's length, and one paragraph summary of the proposed book. Next, tell who you think will be interested in your novel, and why. Briefly describe the plot. (Did the butler do it?) Authors should also tell about themselves, qualifications for writing the book, any literary successes during their writing career, their availability to help market the book. These are only brief summaries of guidelines for developing queries and book proposals. Libraries and bookstores are better sources for serious editor surveys and queries. My track record of sixty-seven rejections during my early submissions experience does not qualify me as an expert in this area of authorship.

Aiming for a new world record for publisher rejection slips with my *Pete* book, I continued pumping out queries as long as the library's L.M.P. supplied new publisher names, the post office didn't run out of stamps, and our bank account didn't go N.S.F. paying for them. Admittedly, my thick skinned armor protecting my ego began to wear microscopically thin in the wrong places. On my worst days I felt shattered as a pinata at a Mexican fiesta. Throughout all the negative feedback, it became increasingly difficult to maintain coherent emotional stability. Perhaps it was time to kick back, analyze the ceiling while steepling my ten fingers, and apply brutal reality to my analysis of the book's merit. I received so many "no thank you's," I wondered, was it possible my personal masterpiece was a dud? Not dissuaded, my commitment to the project, to Pete's memory, pushed me onward. I wondered what words of wisdom he would pass along were he here. Then I remembered one of his favorite maxims, "If at first you don't succeed, to hell with it, go fishing." A tempting cop-out at this low point in my waning writing career.

Cogitating my next strategy, I reviewed several rejection slips from the growing mountain of paper turndowns. A few stated the publisher only accepted submissions from literary agents. Aha! I shouted. That's what I need—a good agent.

Back to the library's L.M.P. book, and the section listing literary agents and addresses. By now I was on a first-name basis with these nice library people.

"Good morning, Ron, how is your book coming along?" asked the prim and proper librarian. This was the fourth time she had asked. My reply was unchanged.

"Hi, Mary, I think I'm close to signing a contract with a publisher." Yeah, I'm about as close as Murmansk is to Miami.

I scribbled down the names and addresses of 10-12 likely sounding agents on the back of one of my printed rejection notices. At least they were good for something. Re-reading one of the publisher guideline books, I boned up on how to query a literary agent. I only jotted down names of agents accepting multiple submissions as identified in the listing. If I fiddled around and limited my barrage of queries to one agent at a time, then waited weeks for the reply, I was fearful that given my track record with publishers, I'd be "down there" with Pete before finding representation.

Buoyed by this new tactic, I finally machine-gunned a dozen queries to agents all over the country. This would be the way to go. Why hadn't I thought of this before? Then the waiting began. One week, two weeks, at the end of the third week, my first reply arrived. It came in my SASE. But that was o.k., they probably used my envelope to request that I send them the entire manuscript.

I found it very strange these literary agents must order their printed rejection forms from the same printer the publishers use. Several had near-identical looking "Sorry" forms. A slight glimmer of hope brightened my day when I read one literary agent's reply: "We like the theme of your book and are willing to read a sample chapter of no more than 25-pages. Please remit fifty-dollars reading fee with your submission." Desperate as I was to find an agent I didn't send the requested payment. Did they think I'd just fallen off the recycled newspaper truck? Instead I sent them a letter stating I'd appreciate their reading a sample chapter but was reluctant to pay for it. There came no reply. I had read in one of the literary books that legitimate agents who were honestly interested in a manuscript would seldom require a reading fee. Just my luck! A positive reply with a negative stipulation.

Receiving no encouraging input from literary agents, I began to worry perhaps my *Pete* book was just not of sufficient quality, and not interesting enough to ever succeed in the competitive book arenas. This realization came with painful honesty and trampled my ego like a martial arts instructor pouncing on a mugger with both feet. I thought *Pete* was a good read; Kit said she enjoyed "most" chapters; my editor reported it had some strengths, a few weaknesses. So there, at least three of us liked it.

From the day I put the first words on paper, I'd assumed that somewhere, sometime, someone would snap up my manuscript, pay me maybe not a small fortune, and publish *Pete*. What was taking them so long? I'd never considered self-publishing. Maybe it was time to think about that.

During my period of cogitation in early summer of 1994, I received an unsolicited, four-page letter from Northwest Publishing, Inc. (NPI), in Salt Lake City. I read it, then read it several more times. It sounded so authentic, so honest and acceptable that it triggered the alarm bell on my conservative wariness. That company had to have an angle and I was determined to find it.

My first concern was how NPI obtained my name. They were one of the few publishers in our vast land that I had not queried. How could I have missed them? I tried to prove to my own satisfaction that NPI was not a "vanity press."

Their opening letter contained all the statements that appealed to budding authors:

"...our modern Salt Lake City facility...perform all aspects of quality book publishing. Our editorial plan...175 to 220 books per year...selected from hundreds of unsolicited manuscripts. Those deemed inappropriate...returned immediately ...NPI seeks to publish only works with outstanding potential ...if your manuscript is selected...a contract will be prepared ...including payments you will receive...royalties paid twice annually. NPI marketing/sales staff will begin promoting your book several months in advance. Descriptive material...mailed to hundreds of book dealers.

—Signed, Jim Van Treese, Publisher

How could I lose? I immediately queried NPI with a brief description, mentioned the 480-double-spaced pages, about 110,000 words. I received a prompt reply, "Yes, we'd like to see your manuscript." Whoopee! At last an interested publisher, but I remained cautious.

I speculated, what the heck. It won't hurt to send them the manuscript just to see what happens. I bundled it up, mailed it first-class even though they suggested more expensive overnight shipping.

In early August, I received a glowing letter from the S.L. publisher. In retrospect the tone was repetitive in several of the "sales" letters from Van Treese: "The marketplace looks good for this type of book, (I'll bet he told everybody that), and with a nice four-color cover that is properly done, it should do real well." I remained suspicious. If it's too good to be true, it usually is.

Within a week I received a phone call from Todd Vacher, Acquisitions Manager at NPI. His message was, "Let me congratulate you for being accepted by NPI as a soon to be published book author."

I restrained my wild enthusiasm. It had all been too easy. "What happens next?" I asked Vacher.

"We will mail you a contract today for your review and subsequent signing," he told me.

I remained quite cautious when I told Kit, "That publisher in Salt Lake City tells me they've accepted my book manuscript. Let's not buy the celebration champagne until we review the agreement coming in the mail."

The six-page contract arrived the next day. Impressive. It came Overnight Federal Express. I read, then re-read those six pages at least a dozen times trying to find the "hook." Then I discovered Point 1.5.1 on page two that proved to be the clinker:

"The publisher will print 10,000 copies of the book, present a direct mail sales effort to 2,000 bookstores, promote it at the annual American Bookseller's Convention, test market 2,500 copies, and pursue other publication options."

Those words were so beautiful to the ego of a first-time author that I felt guilty about my ongoing suspicions of NPI.

Guess I should have listened more closely to my suspicious side.

Then came the "hook:" "For these services the publisher will pay half of the expenses, bill the author for 50%, namely $6,125.00. Included will be 100 free copies of the book."

I calculated, if they would do everything stated in the contract, *and if* I could bump the 100 free books up to 1,000 copies, it might be acceptable. If they're going to print 10,000 books, they could well-afford to give me another 900, or so I surmised. My line of reasoning was that each book would then cost me $6.13, with a retail price (NPI suggested) of $9.95. Heck, I could sell 1,000 copies of *Pete* if they would accept my proposal. In my naivete, I'd overlooked the need to wholesale the book at around 50% of retail. My only alternative would have been for me to stand on the street corner and peddle the thousand books at full retail price. Not likely.

Lesson learned, #196.

Enthusiastic, but still suspicious, I ran the NPI contract past an attorney specializing in book publishing legalities. The lawyer suggested revising the contract to agree to the $6,125.00 payment, *but* I pay 50% up front, the balance upon delivery of 1,000 books, and proof the publisher had met the other contractual stipulations. I further decided I'd offer to deposit the remaining balance into an escrow account at a Salt Lake financial institution selected by the publisher. The bank would pay NPI the escrow balance upon satisfactory proof of performance.

Ha! With those modifications, I'd have them exactly where they wanted me.

Taking the proposal one more step, I ordered a complete credit report on the publishing firm. Surprisingly, it came back quite positive. "The company paid their bills as timely as 80% of other firms in the same business." There had been several judgements against NPI but all had been satisfied.

At this point I called NPI's Todd Vacher and told him about my proposed contract revisions.

"I don't see any problems with those stipulations," Vacher replied. "Let me run them past Mr. Van Treese and I'll get back to you." His quick agreement surprised me like I'd just won the poker pot without even holding a pair.

Within the hour he called and reported, "We don't have any objections. Go ahead and have your attorney modify the contract. You sign and return it along with your check covering half of your half of the expenses."

"Where do you want me to deposit the escrow money for the second payment?" I inquired, very businesslike.

"We don't think that will be necessary, Ron, we trust you'll pay the balance after we do our part," he replied. "After all, we put a lot of emphasis on trust in this business." I was astonished at their acceptance of my terms, and then not wanting an escrow deposit. As I'm sure it was intended, this nonchalance and indifference towards money gave me a feeling of confidence and reduced my wariness with NPI. Unfortunately, I didn't realize I was the lamb being led to the woodshed.

NPI's contract specified 365 days for them to fulfill their obligations, including the 1,000 gratis books. Initially I balked at such a long-term contract, but relented upon learning that one-year for publication was about the norm in the industry.

"At this time there are more than 100 authored books ahead of you awaiting the syndication process," Vacher said. "We publish strictly on a first signed contract basis. I couldn't move yours up without disappointing a lot of other authors," he concluded. The lamb was fast approaching the woodshed.

I signed, mailed the contract along with my check on Sept. 7, 1994. I had told Vacher that Kit and I had planned a Midwest vacation and hoped to swing into Salt Lake City around September 12th. I wanted to see their facility, meet both Vacher and Van Treese. He agreed to our schedule.

Earlier, I snooped through several bookstores trying to find books published by NPI. They had sent me a long and impressive list of recent titles and authors, itemizing almost 300 books they had printed. I found several, but not in great quantities. The printing quality of the few I located seemed to be quite acceptable.

Arriving at Salt Lake City, we were impressed with the size of the NPI facility which we toured with Vacher as our guide. He reminded me a bit of a used car salesman, but Kit says I am always too critical. I should have been more so.

Jim Van Treese had an unimpressive office, seemed friendly, dressed as I remember in western cowboy garb. But who doesn't in Utah? He was probably in his early fifties, gave us the vague feeling he was too busy to spend much time with us. One of his sons was in the office and surprisingly talked about his dad in less than complimentary tones. I had the welcome opportunity to meet some of the department people, putting faces on voices I'd talked with on the phone.

Back at our motel that night Kit and I exchanged impressions and opinions about NPI.

"Van Treese seemed like your typical good old boy, and I wonder about his cowboy clothes and junky office?" Kit volunteered.

"The entire place looked messy," I opined, "but everyone seemed busy and they are certainly printing books." We came away without strong positive or negative feelings about NPI or their management people.

Acknowledging NPI's one-year contract, I realized it could be awhile before the *Pete* book came off the press. I began planning for my second major writing project. Remembering the interviews, research and short stories I had done on the Northwest outlaw, John Tornow, this seemed like a logical subject for my next book.

Every couple of months, I called NPI to determine if *Pete* had been placed in the publishing queue. Unlike the home on the range, seldom did I hear an encouraging word. I worried when their departmental supervisors began mysteriously disappearing like antagonists in the former Soviet KGB. Six months into our twelve-month publishing lag, I called one day to once again harass Todd Vacher.

"I'm sorry, he's no longer here," came the unfamiliar receptionist's reply. I was assigned a new contact person, Sally Davis, Editor-In-Chief. I was satisfied. She seemed quite personable, knowledgable, and assured me that NPI was progressing on *Pete*. Following Vacher's departure, the twenty-some photos I'd sent with the manuscript came up missing. Sally initiated an NPI search which eventually located the missing pictures.

Contractually, by September, 1995 NPI should have printed, published and promoted *Pete*, and I should have received my 1,000 gratis books. When none of these events occurred, I wrote Van Treese a scathing letter advising him his contract had expired. "What's goin' on?"

My red-hot communique evidently rattled someone's C.R.T. in S.L.C. Within a week I received galley proofs for the book along with instructions for marking and returning. Now I had another new contact person, Joshua Parsons, Editor. These guys changed personnel as often as Indy 500 racers changed tires. Within two days I'd read and returned the proofs, reminding Parsons that NPI was a month overdue on fulfilling my contract. A minor concern was the galley printing which seemed to be in a confusing, scrunched up type that was hard to read. They said not to worry, it would be o.k. on the final run. I was beginning to visualize wings flying my three grand over the Tabernacle in Salt Lake City.

I initiated numerous contacts with NPI during late 1995 and early 1996 to no avail. Then, in April, 1996, an experience never forgotten, the roof caved in. I received a bankruptcy court notification that NPI was in Chapter Seven. There was some rather harsh language in the official document and other notifications I received later:

"To date the trustee has discovered that over a period of four years, the principals of the debtor (NPI) cashed 4,587 checks made payable to Northwest Publishing, Inc. in the total amount of $10,283,778.91 at a check cashing business and have failed to account for this cash."

"The trustee filed a complaint against James Van Treese and Jason Van Treese early in 1996. The complaint seeks recovery from these two individuals in the amount of at least $10,500,000 based upon defendants' corporate mismanagement of Northwest Publishing, Inc. and upon fact showing that Northwest Publishing was really the alter ego of the Van Treeses. In addition, the trustee continues to cooperate with various governmental agencies investigating potential criminal matters related to this debtor."

The investigation resulted in a state court criminal action being filed against both James and Jason Van Treese.

Reading these reports it became painfully obvious my enthusiasm and my checkbook had marched ahead of my conservative wariness and common sense. Perhaps my experience will instill in others utmost vigilance to be alert when confronted with similar, tempting "opportunities."

Following the demise of NPI, I envisioned one last glimpse of my $3M check winging over Utah's Wasatch Mountains with Van Treese astride it like a bronc rider, both man and money riding off into the sunset. I felt lower than an angleworm's belly button.

Lesson #197. Don't contribute funds to suspicious characters who might take your dough and ride off into the sunset.

Chapter 4

Kit was gentle with me. No loud words; no, "I told you so;" not even any wisecracks about what we might do with the celebratory champagne we had bought prematurely. About her only comment was, "That's too bad. Now what will you do with the manuscript?"

That was the question, the question of the moment. Where do I go with my cherished 480-typed pages, my 110,000-words? Quite a few publishers had already told me where I could go with them. But, I had too many hours, expenses, and lemon tree legal pads invested to just chuck the whole megillah. Besides, I had confidence the book had at least minimal value. Somehow I needed to jumpstart my enthusiasm. I wasn't quite down for the count, but neither was I anxious to climb back into the ring.

"You shouldn't allow NPI's floundering to cast negative shadows on your work," Kit counseled. "NPI went kaput from their own doing, not from anything you did."

I knew she was right, and was trying to soothe my badly bruised ego with empathy and a sound perception.

"Maybe I should investigate the feasibility of self-publishing." I ran that possibility up the conversational flag pole to see if it would draw any fire from my evaluator.

"Sure, why don't you?" was my wife's favorable response.

Where to start? I'd seen ads—even received proposals from several small-to-medium-sized printing/publishing houses.

There had been numerous mailed catalogs from "vanity publishers" whose primary mission was to profit from printing books by authors anxious to see their name in print. I believe legitimate book printers try to produce first-class work at an acceptable price. In retrospect, NPI closely fit the "vanity publisher" description. They just did a better job of disguising their true profit motive with smoke and mirrors.

Surprisingly, answers from a few of my original queries to publishers were continuing to dribble back in, months later, but nothing very encouraging. One reply apologized for his tardiness, excusing it with, "I've been out of the country for several months." I had mailed a query to him almost a year earlier.

In self-publishing, my greatest concern was finding just the right printer—one I'd feel comfortable with—one who cranked out quality at a reasonable price. I talked with several printing houses sprinkled around the U.S. Coming from ground zero in modern printing knowledge, I realized I needed to locate a firm that would gently lead me down the most productive printing path, not another trip to the woodshed.

While flipping through "Writer's Northwest" tabloid newspaper one day, I spotted an ad for a printer located close to home in tiny Rochester, Washington.

"That would make sense," I told Kit. "Communicating with a local firm would be much easier. If a nose-to-nose meeting became necessary, I could be there within an hour."

That day in June '96, my call to Gorham Printing kicked off a successful business relationship which I'm certain will endure down through the years.

Being somewhat frugal (Kit says I'm just cheap), I noted with satisfaction that Gorham Printing offered a toll-free phone number. Just a tiny quirk, but I'm more liable to contact a business with a freebie phone number than one requiring me to spend my own nickel. Yes, Virginia, once a phone call was a nickel, later it went to a dime, then 15-cents for a short time, next a quarter, now thirty-five cents.

I called Kurt Gorham, owner, president, CEO, chairman-of-the board, for Gorham Printing. I asked for an appointment to talk about printing my book with him. Obtaining a mutually-agreeable time was easy, getting directions to find his print shop was more difficult, much more difficult.

I thought it would be easy. The town of Rochester is a three-block-long conglomeration of small businesses sprawled along State Route Twelve. Anything, even a nickel, should be a piece of cake to find in Rochester. But not Gorham Printing, at least not easily.

"Where are you located in Rochester?" I asked. My query necessitated nearly a full, yellow-page sheet to scribble down the verbal map he gave me over the phone. It seemed that Rochester was only a beginning point, not the actual location of this ink and paper business. It almost came down to: "Take the one-lane gravel road leading through the dark, spooky forest. After a few miles you'll see a small brown cow (*not* the black and white one) drinking from a murky, green creek. Turn left there and go..."

If Gorham had been distilling illegal spirits, they couldn't have located in a more secluded neck of the woods.

On the appointed day, with reserve fuel, extra tires just in case, and several updated Rand McNallys, I struck out to find Gorham Printing. Only the black and white cow was drinking, but I turned there anyway. Without much trouble I soon arrived at the farm-setting of the Gorham print shop.

I found it pleasingly quiet in the woodsy place, out there where it's easy to be one with the land, so tranquil and unhurried. This was as fine a slice of real estate as I'd ever set tires on. I realized why Kurt chose the remoteness.

The weary old, one-eyed shaggy dog stiffly stood up from napping on the porch and greeted me with a deep, un-scary, *woof-woof.* This signal alerted Kurt who met me at the door of his small office, adjacent to a large room chock-full of presses and various printing equipment that would have sent Johannes Gutenberg into an ecstatic orbit.

Kurt was tall, sandy-hair, beaming a broad welcoming smile highlighted by his sparkling eyes that fairly danced with enthusiasm. My snap judgment immediately told me this guy was cable-ready and I was going to like him.

"Come in and I'll give you a tour of the place, messy though it is," he said.

You can usually recognize a business that is thriving, or one that is hurting for customers. Gorham Printing had piles of printed material, and boxes of printed books stacked against the wall. The press was cranking out a "sixteen-up" flat sheet operated by a young printer in jeans who gave the impression he might have just come in from milking the cows. One other employee was running a collator-type machine, folding pages into book form. The clank, clatter and whirring of the equipment emitted sounds of busy-ness and productivity. "This place is humming," I said to Kurt, raising my voice above the machine noise. "I just love the aroma of a print shop, the ink, the paper, whatever combines to make up that smell."

"It's what we have flowing in our veins," Kurt smiled, "we get a transfusion with each new book."

"Well, you certainly look busy here. Are you sure you can handle another printing job?"

"Right now we're running a bit behind, but we'll catch up in a week or so. We try to schedule a six-week leadtime," he said, waving a blue, ink-stained hand at the stacks of printed pages.

Following our tour and my snide remarks alluding to his location (he said they wanted to stay out of the high-rent district), we discussed book printing. I had a zillion questions.

"Could he print b & w pics from color?"

"No problem."

"Could he reproduce this color picture of me and Pete for the cover?"

"Sure, my artist, Kathy Campbell can."

"Can you do two, or three-color covers?"

"We do it all the time."

"Can you steer me in the right direction for obtaining ISBN number, Library of Congress listing, copyrights and bar code information?"

"That's what we're here for," Kurt answered casually.

When we got around to talking cost of books, Kurt handed me a small catalog that answered most of my monetary questions. The booklet lists sizes, number of pages, various quantity brackets, and how they handled pictures and illustrations.

Kurt confirmed my logical suspicion that quantity of books ordered was a major deciding factor in arriving at a price.

On a cost per book comparison, in most sizes, ordering 500 books would be nearly double the price per book compared with ordering 3,000 books. I felt comfortable talking with the print shop owner. He gave me the impression he wouldn't promise anything he couldn't deliver.

I found a noticeable difference between Gorham and other printers contacted regarding their desire to assist customers and do whatever was needed to stay within an author's budget. I had questioned other printing establishments, "Can you do...?"

"Well, that will be more costly."

"Then, could you...?"

"Well, that will require more time and money."

Gorham's seemed to be a "can-do," customer-oriented business, a business aimed at total satisfaction.

I had my *Pete* book in hard-copy manuscript form and also captured on disk by my whiz-bang Brother apparatus. I'm still overwhelmed by the technology. All 480-pages were on that tiny disk.

Planning strategy with Kurt and his printing people, I decided to go 6x9, perfect-bound, three color cover, and shoot for a total of 208-pages. Later, as they "read" my disk, Kurt reported *Pete* was too wordy, it would never fit into 208-pages.

Tongue-in-cheek, he told me, "You'll have to give away a magnifying glass with each book so buyers can read the tiny print."

We finally settled on a 256-page edition, larger type, producing a very readable book, even for old folks.

How many to print? Always the big decision for wordsmiths to ponder. How popular will it be? How wide a distribution?

What retail price? How much support will your book receive from the media? A long press-run provides more books, at a cheaper price per book but a possibility of the writer getting "stuck" with unsaleable books. On shorter press-runs, there is a higher price per book, but you may run out of books before the market has been satisfied. Decisions, decisions.

My conservative nature flipped *Pete* into the latter classification. Turned down by so many publishers and agents, I feared the hard reality was that the book would not appeal to the general public. Besides, as my subconscious elfin muse often reminded me, "This one's for Pete's memory, and to get your feet wet in the self-publishing game. You're not concerned with profit."

I'm not? Well, no, I guess I'm not really profit-minded on this one.

Contracts between authors/printers often stipulate the customer will accept under/over-runs on final book quantities. With Gorham Printing the over-runs were at a lesser price than the ordered quantity. I received 540 copies on an order of 500 *Pete* books. Even though the forty books were less expensive per book than the five-hundred, the entire lot came to an individual book cost of $7.38. I wholesaled them at $5.00, and retailed at $9.95. Ninety-five percent were sold at wholesale. With this tremendous profit I don't understand why everyone isn't writing and self-publishing books!

Lesson #198. Don't overlook wholesale vs. retail.

I should have ordered a thousand books instead of five-hundred (I even thought I had before looking it up for writing this book). My cost would have been approximately $1.50 less per book. Pete sold out in just a few months, and there wouldn't have been any trouble selling a thousand books. Many buyers were disappointed. Isn't hindsight always 20-20?

Pete's retail price of $9.95 was too low for a 256-page, 110,000-word (quality?) book. It would've sold easily at $13.95.

Lesson #199. Don't underprice your "best-seller."

Perhaps one of the most important decisions a self-publisher will make is cover layout, color and illustrations. When I see a book with a ho-hum, white cover displaying nothing more than printed words, I'm usually not motivated to buy it. Maybe the old axiom, "You can't judge a book by it's cover," applies in some situations. But national manufacturers spend millions designing packaging for their wares that literally scream out, "Pick me up and take me home." Book covers often visually "sell" the book.

I wanted a picture on the cover of *Pete* that would denote and project the title, *Me N' Pete.* I had only one good picture of the two of us in an outdoor setting. It was perfect for the cover: Outdoorsy, which the book was about; with me holding two, nice-sized trout, Pete holding a fly-fishing rod; both of us grinning like a couple of chessycats which portrayed the humor, the book's mainstay. The pair of us typified the book's name. Wrap it up in outdoor colors, green and brown—we had our cover.

Gorham's technology and professional staff produce a high-quality book at a reasonable price to the author. His illustrator, Kathy Campbell, displayed unlimited patience with me as I nit-picked several mock-ups of the cover design. I groused, "The 'N' between 'Me' and 'Pete' should be smaller and better spaced. The proof copy looks like "Men Pete." Sixty-five miles away over the phone, I envisioned Kathy rolling her eyes to the ceiling as she unflappably pumped out another and another proof of the cover. The final was perfect, although we never totally agreed on where the comma belonged when substituting just "N" for "And". Should it be N', or 'N? We settled on N'. Later I learned it should be 'N'.

There seems to be a variety of binding available, each with a different price, and intended for specific usage. I selected "perfect binding" for *Pete,* primarily because I knew absolutely nothing about it, and that binding was recommended by Kurt. It's middle-road, price-wise, and seems to be the basic paperback book binding. The wraparound cover is bound to the pages with hot, flexible glue. From the ultimate total of 5,000 books printed, separation at the binding was almost nonexistent.

Another decision, among many, is the size of book desired. Gorham prints just about any size, but the popular, and most-efficient sizes for reduced paper waste are 5½x8½, 6x9, and 8½x11. Standard pocketbook, mass-market size seems to be 4x6¾, (all in inches). One consideration on selecting size might be where the book will be merchandised, if at all, at retail. I chose 6x9 for Pete, classified as "trade paperback," but found it too large to fit on the smaller pocketbook racks. This could have been either a plus, or a negative.

If it wouldn't fit the smaller racks, then it wouldn't become lost in the gazillion pocketbooks on today's market. Most retail book outlets have the oversize racks that accommodate limited quantities of the 6x9'ers. Any self-publishers planning to market in a variety of locations should pre-plan book size.

It would seem that writing the book should be the most difficult task. Not so, no siree. There's a multitude of "small details" needing attention by the self-publisher before the manuscript is put to bed. To be more specific, things I needed like Copyright consideration; application for an ISBN number; submission of a listing for the "Books In Print" catalog; obtaining a bar-code for the new "baby," and applying for a Library Of Congress Catalog Card number. Any print shop worth its black ink will help authors slice through the red tape and paperwork of these necessities.

ISBN. The International Standard Book Numbering system is voluntary. So says the information sheet supplied by R.R. Bowker, the ISBN agency. Hah! Just try to get a newly published book off the ground without the all-important number. All distributors, all major booksellers, and some smaller retailers won't even talk with you unless you have the hallowed ciphers. I filled out a Bowker form supplied by Gorham's, mailed it with my check for $115.00, and within a few weeks received a block of ten, ISBN numbers. Only expecting one number this was a pleasant surprise. Now I can write six or seven more books free of an ISBN fee after I use my first three, or four numbers. Although it was a bit spendy, this was the only expense I encountered among all the registration and applications that enabled the book to be counted among the other new books. The fee has probably increased since I registered in 1996.

The ISBN Agency's mailing address is: R.R. Bowker, 121 Chanlon Road, New Providence, NJ 07974, Phone (908) 665 6770.

COPYRIGHT. I was told that the act of printing, maybe even typing the original manuscript constituted copyrighting my material. Unpublished works, or authors demanding ironclad copyright protection can register with the Copyright Office. Their hotline number is (202) 707 3000.

LIBRARY OF CONGRESS CATALOG CARD NUMBER. These numbers are issued prior to publication and are then printed on the copyright page of the new book along with the copyright symbol and statement. It is a book identification number used mostly by libraries and will be issued by writing: Cataloging in Publications Division, The Library of Congress, Washington, DC 20540-4320.

Their hotline is (202) 707-6346. These folks will appreciate receiving a gratis copy of your book when it is published.

BOOKS IN PRINT. R.R. Bowker also publishes several voluminous editions of this titled listing which identifies every book in print in the U.S., and is complimentarily updated annually.

The tiny print chronicle can be found in libraries, and is touted as, "The most important bibliographic resource in which you can have your titles correctly represented."

BOOKLAND BAR CODE. The International ISBN agency and the International Article Numbering System (EAN) have collaborated to establish the ISBN/Bookland EAN bar code. The printing houses have access to the code which can be scanned by booksellers to determine the book's correct selling price, etc. It works much like the multitude of bar codes (i.e. supermarket) where the cashier's scanner reads the code on each product purchased, along with the store's individual selling price. Then when you arrive home and read your cash register tape you know how much you paid for those corn flakes and other goodies.

Notwithstanding my wholesale grocery background, I bumped into a problem with this book bar code thing. The bars printed on the back of *Pete* couldn't be scanned by the supermarket front ends. I was told that Bookland bars were indigenous to booksellers, and become illiterate to other retail scanning systems. Books distributed only through bookstores will do fine with the Bookland bars. We made everyone happy the old-fashioned way on the *Pete* book. We printed the actual selling price ($9.95) beside the Bookland Bar Code. This worked satisfactorily nearly everywhere with the possible exception being south of Ohanepecosh where I'd heard the locals sometimes experienced difficulty reading English.

One other bar code glitch to be aware of. We sold *Pete* in many supermarkets. Nearly all products in the markets are controlled through their computer system. When merchandise arrives, it is added to the inventory. When sold, it is deducted from the inventory. The bar codes provide this tracking system. But not being able to "read" the Bookland Bars, the markets had no tracking for sales of my book. They could have developed a system to control the books, but it would have been more time consuming than it was worth.

* * *

With a handshake Kurt Gorham and I reached agreement on printing five-hundred copies of *Me N' Pete*. I needed to consolidate the chapters onto one disk, then determine if the format was compatible with the Gorham system. Kurt had already begun developing the book's cover design. He also supplied forms/addresses for obtaining the necessary documents and registrations.

Getting all the loose nuts and bolts organized, I wrote Kurt a deposit check on July 30, 1996 for half the total printing cost. He began serious work on my manuscript, my first printed book. The production schedule allowed 4-6 weeks before delivery.

At the time of contract signing, I felt like the little Dutch boy—twelve holes in the dike—only ten fingers.

I was attempting to finish several promised stained glass projects, another diversion I'd started as a sideline, but just for friends and neighbors. My second book was nearly finished. It depicted the humorous and exciting experiences Kit and I encountered during our seven-week volunteer project in St. Petersburg, Russia. I'd also begun my rewrite of John Tornow's life and times.

Pausing for a few moments one day, I suddenly realized there would soon be five-hundred *Pete* books on my doorstep and I had not even a clue what to do with them. Oh, oh, time to sit down at the drawing board, sit down and devise a plan for sales and distribution of my new "baby."

Well, let's see now, Kit had promised to buy one. Then there were a few dependable friends, but I disliked twisting arms to sell something to friends and neighbors.

Pete and I had several mutual grocer acquaintances who owned supermarkets in Western Washington. I contacted Chuck and Mark Swanson, and Chris Pickering, who agreed to hold book signings in their stores. Chuck was a enthusiastic promoter because one of the book's chapters described an Alaskan fishing trip where he was one of the main characters.

I arranged to sell the $9.95 retail books to the stores at a wholesale cost of $5.00. By making it profitable for the grocers they bought advertising space in the local newspapers, promoting the book. The publicity announced the kickoff of the *Pete* book, along with my picture and the scheduled dates and times for the signings. How many would we sell??

Chapter 5

Later that autumn afternoon, after setting up the schedules with the grocers, I pointed Cherokee toward home. It was one of those glorious fall days so revered in our far Northwest corner of the U.S. I mentally rambled through my checklist of tasks necessary to achieve the successful book signings at the supermarkets. This pensive itemizing was suddenly interrupted by Cherokee's beeping radar detector, causing a reflex action of removing my foot from gas pedal.

Aha, there he is perched on his straddle-rocket, wearing his brain-cage helmet, lurking in the bushes beside the freeway. The state patrol motorcycle cops cover this stretch of highway like a blanket on a four-poster.

With a smile at reduced legal speed, I passed the patrolman, but resisted the temptation to immediately resume my faster speed. Motorcycle cops are like bumblebees—you seldom see just one. I didn't want to meet his buddy with a ticket book further down the road.

Arriving home, feeling I'd accomplished a great coup with the scheduled *Pete* book signings, I began planning how in this wide world I could sell the remainder of those books. This was not the proper procedure as learned in Business 101, not the proper procedure at all. First you determine the market, then you develop the product. I was going at it bassackwards, putting the bookstore ahead of the book, so to speak.

Bookstores! That's the answer to my gnawing enigma, I suddenly discovered, almost spilling hot coffee on my newly-pressed pants. I needed to pre-plan sales through the bookstores, sit back and wait for the profits to roll in. Profits? Oh, oh, how much would they pay me for a book retailing at $9.95 that cost me over seven-dollars? Oh well, profit was no big deal. It's the experience that counts. But, like Pete used to say, "I hope I can break even on this deal…"

There were several large chain bookstores in our area, Barnes & Noble having the most outlets. They became my target, my bulls-eye for book sales.

I decided to approach the store closest to home in Tacoma, approach it with temerity, shoulders back, head high, posing as a successful author.

By this time I had several final printings of just the *Pete* book cover, three-color, glossy finish. That would become my irresistible sales tool, my piece de resistance.

Digging out my executive vice-president's suit that I hadn't worn in several years, checking for moth holes, I dressed like a prosperous author, or like I imagined a prosperous author should dress. That was in place of my casual, more comfortable Pierre K-Mart wardrobe, jeans and t-shirt.

As I waltzed right up to the first Barnes & Noble clerk I saw, she viewed me quizzically, perhaps even suspiciously.

"Good morning," I chortled. "Who would I talk to about buying books?"

"You want to buy books?" she asked, seeking clarification.

"No, I would like to sell you some books."

"Oh…oh," she stammered, flinching like I'd just struck a blow against literacy. "Perhaps you should talk with our manager. Let me get her for you."

Waiting near the front checkout, I became engrossed with the "Fifty-percent off" selection table when I noticed a stylishly-dressed woman approaching me. Her hand was extended as if to dispel any thought she was against shaking hands with a man. (Some are, you know.)

"I'm the store manager, how can I be of assistance?" she asked in a pleasant, lilting voice.

"I'm Ron Fowler, local author of a soon-to-be published humorous outdoor book covering thirty-five years of hunting, hiking, fishing escapades in the Pacific Northwest. I'd like to solicit your interest in my book, perhaps arrange to place it in your inventory." Gasping for breath after rattling off my sales pitch, trying to say it all in fifteen-seconds, I also flashed the shiny Gorham-printed book cover at her. I don't think she noticed it one whit.

For a brief second the manager said nothing. It was quite obvious that her cerebral gears were engaged and composing an appropriate reply. Soon, in a tone that sounded policy-approved she trilled, "We try to support local authors whenever we can. Who will be distributing your book?"

Beaming in self-satisfaction, I replied with confidence disproportionate to my chances of literary survival, "Oh, I will."

"You're the author *and* the distributor?"

Nodding in the affirmative, I wondered, what's the big deal about doing both, being both word-slinger and also deliveryman.

Backing off just a bit, she began enunciating very slowly, very succinctly, like I was the third-grade pupil, she the schoolmarm. "We must procure all books through authorized distributors. Barnes & Noble cannot buy books from just anybody who comes through the door."

"How do I become an authorized distributor?"

"Perhaps our regional procurement office can assist you," she replied. "Let me give you a name and phone number."

Lesson #200. You gotta have a distributor.

Right after breakfast the next day I called the B & N regional buyer in Costa Mesa, California explaining I wanted to get my *Pete* book into the local B & N stores so I could schedule signings and readings with them. I think we bypassed a mile of red tape requiring forms, sample books, perhaps a vote by members of the board, and many weeks of time, if I had been trying for authorization in multiple B & N outlets.

"If you're only thinking about local stores in your immediate area, I can authorize that," the pleasant speaking, cooperative buyer told me. "But you will still need to ship through one of our authorized distributors."

The buyer gave me names and addresses over the phone for three authorized distributors. Scribbling furiously, I recognized the first name as a company the rumor mill predicted would soon be out of business. The second, a well-known distributor, was located about 250-miles from Tacoma. A phone call to them confirmed my suspicion that I'd have to pay freight to their warehouse. That didn't seem very plausible when I knew, for instance, a distributor would probably pay me at least two dollars per book less than my cost.

I gazed upwards and quietly whispered to Pete, "I just wish I *could* break even on this dumb book deal of ours. How did I ever let you shame me into this?"

I'd never heard of the third name, and wondered about the size of the organization; Wolverine Distributors, Charley Soames, Basin, Wyoming. Where in hell was Basin, Wyoming? Peering intently through my magnifying glass at a Wyoming map, I finally spotted it. There it was, between Manderson and Graybull. Everybody should know that. But, it was my last chance to get *Pete* into Barnes & Noble. So I called Wolverine. It rang once.

"Charley here," boomed out over the phone, sounding exactly like I'd expect someone to sound from Basin, Wyoming. No receptionist? I wondered if it was a one-person operation.

I boomed right back, "Charley, my name is Ron Fowler, I live near Tacoma, and they tell me you hold the key to getting my soon-to-be published book into the Barnes and Noble stores."

"They told you right," he said, or words to that effect.

Mr. Soames' voice was chunky like the phone call had caught him eating a candy bar, or something.

Hesitating in disbelief, I asked, "What's the procedure?"

"Well, it's fairly easy. You ship your books express to me, then the Barnes and Noble stores can order from my inventory, or if you have a signed order from the store, FAX it to me and I'll fill it. Then I express the books to the stores."

"Do any of the Tacoma-area B & N stores order from you now?" I asked in astonishment. "Also, I assume I have to pay shipping expenses to your warehouse."

"Yes, the inbound freight is your responsibility. I don't think any of the stores in your area buy from us, but they could. We'd just express the books to them."

While sipping my third cup of coffee, I thought about this suggested procedure for a few seconds, then replied, "Charley, I have an aversion toward inefficiency and this plan doesn't make a lot of sense to me, especially in my situation."

From the tone of his voice I could determine he wasn't happy with my critique. "What's wrong with it?"

"Here I am in Tacoma. The most distant B & N store I want to do business with is twenty-miles away, one is only three-miles away. You're suggesting I send my books all the way to Wyoming, probably close to a thousand miles. In turn you will ship books to the stores, another thousand-mile trip. That's around two thousand-miles while I could accomplish the same distribution in twenty-miles. Charley, the handling is going to wear the print off those books. Isn't there a simpler method?"

"Yes, I see your point. I didn't know you would only want books distributed to those few stores in close proximity to Tacoma. Let me think for a moment."

There were a few moments of silence. I agitated about the long-distance phone bill, then remembered I'd used Charley's freebie 800 number.

The silence was broken by, "Are you still there?"

"I'm here, lay it on me Charley."

"That company has allowed me a seldom-used drop shipment program. You would deliver the books, obtain a signed receipt, ship the paperwork to me, and I would invoice their headquarters office. I'd pay you for the books in about sixty-days. Does that sound better?"

"It sounds a lot more efficient. What amount would I receive for a book retailing at $9.95?"

I could hear Charley mumbling as he calculated the amount. Evidently it was a set percentage, no room for negotiating, take it or leave it.

"You'll receive $4.48 for each book," he told me.

Ten Western Washington daily and weekly newspapers ran feature articles on John Tornow and the book that chronicled his life.

Hearing this took my breath away like I'd just been compressed in a Wyoming cattle-squeezer.

"You're paying me less than half the retail price," I blurted out.

"Sorry, that's the book business. We all have to make a living. You might want to check with the B & N stores, make sure they can still use this drop-ship program."

I thanked him, told the Wyoming entrepreneur that I'd check it out and get back to him. I was still in dollar-shock from learning I'd lose around three-dollars for every book Barnes & Noble sold. Maybe if I was lucky, they wouldn't sell many. No, that didn't equate either.

The three Barnes & Noble stores approved the drop-ship program. We agreed to do business when the books became available from Gorham Printing.

This suggested two-thousand mile round-trip for my books was indicative of several other inefficiencies and what I'd call just, "dumb procedures" I discovered in the book-selling business. Coming from a wholesale grocery discipline where every minute, every mile, every penny, meant the difference between profit or loss, it was difficult for me to understand these procedures. The inept handling wasn't limited to just a few, it seemed to be the norm in the book industry.

Lesson #201. Double-handling is rather inefficient.

As I began planning marketing and distribution strategy for *Pete*, it became obvious I needed publicity to inform the general public about the book. Newspapers in close proximity to my former hometown responded to my plea for a news story, "...former resident publishes first book."

There are many gimmicks and techniques available to the enterprising author/publisher to obtain both printed and electronic publicity for their work. It requires only persistence, having a story to tell, ingenuity, gobs of shoe-leather, capped off by a pleasant smile and the thick hide of a rhinoceros. I'll cover many of the methods that worked for me in later passages.

I found the grocery supermarkets quite receptive to having book-signings in their stores. It was a win/win for them. They made the retail profit on the books I sold, and the signing brought in customers who would do other shopping while in the stores. The retailers bought the books at wholesale, either from me, or (later) from their authorized distributors.

The supermarkets who controlled their own advertising, as opposed to chain stores, were more than willing to feature my book-signings in their newspaper ads. However, we did obtain placement in several Safeway stores, but without being advertised in their grocery ad. Several independents ran the book title, time and location of the signing, selling price, and often included my picture. Such notoriety!

The larger independent and chain bookstores were also willing to host readings and signings for the same reasons; profit from sales, bringing customers into their stores. Most bookstores have already developed limited publicity programs to inform the public about scheduled readings and signings. Barnes & Noble, among others, does a commendable job of pre-advertising author-sessions in-house, with signs, announcements and bulletins. My primary concern with their on-site advertising is that it only reaches in-store customers, missing the entire general public. Most daily newspapers run a "book events" column publicizing meetings, signings and literary happenings of interest to the reading public, and people in writing clubs and organizations. If given sufficient advance notice the papers will run a short paragraph on upcoming author events. This publicity is minimal, and I found that regular news articles were more effective in developing attendance at the signings/readings. But, we have to accept what is available. In my situation, losing two or three dollars per book didn't leave many bucks for buying advertising.

Lesson #201-B. Publicity is important.

Most of the bookstores designate a person with the responsibility of publicizing their "coming author-events." At Barnes & Noble they are identified as "Community Relations Coordinator." Most CRC's are proficient in maximizing "freebie" news coverage for their events. But I've noticed only the big-name authors receive paid newspaper advertising by the bookstores, which is understandable. Newspaper advertising isn't cheap, but more on that later.

For many years Pete had worked as a salesman for the Schilling/McCormack spice company. I had thought perhaps that firm would want to have some participation with the book. We could have emphasized/advertised Schilling subtly, dedicated the book to "...a faithful Schilling representative." There was even a possibility that Schilling could order at least a gazillion books to give to their good customers, and/or employees. Pete was well-known and well-liked by many friends in the food industry.

I contacted several officials in the Schilling organization for consideration of the book, but they decided not to support, or get involved with *Pete*. I still believe they missed a golden P.R. opportunity. But what do I know? One Schilling official offered to buy a personal copy if I would contact him when it became available. Another milestone. (Millstone?) With his copy, and the ones Kit and Mary had promised to buy, I already had three books pre-sold. Only 497 to go!

At some point in the overall scheme of book business, sellers and major distributors need assurance that a newly-emerging book will interest readers, interest them in sufficient numbers to guarantee sales. Reviewing the criteria in retrospect, I think I was very fortunate with *Pete*. The topic—outdoors in the Northwest—humor, had wide appeal. Another plus, I planned distribution in an area where I had lived for many years, my home stompin' ground. Many people—book readers—knew both me and Pete. The book was moderately priced at $9.95, the low side of the retail scale. A tremendous advantage was the opening "push" given the book by friends in the grocery business when the "baby" was first born.

Although sales movement is a hoped-for attribute, returns are a concern throughout the book distribution chain. For books that don't sell, retailers return to distributors, then distributors back to authors/publishers. But the book stops there. Kurt Gorham is a nice guy, but not nice enough to accept returned books that don't sell.

Pete contained twenty, black and white photos. Later I found it surprising when I observed many people would pick up the book and immediately begin flipping pages, looking for pictures or illustrations. Perhaps seeing photos in a book helps readers to determine what the book is all about. After page-flipping, some would buy it, others would smile, put it down and walk away.

Lesson #202. Include lots of interesting photos.

Within a couple of weeks of approving the final layout, design and cover color, Kurt called to say the galley proofs for the text were ready for proofreading. He popped the 256-pages into the mail and we received them the next day. Kit took half the pages and I grabbed the rest. We each read our portions, then swapped so each of us read the book in its entirety. We found very few errors, although I made some changes that were no fault of Gorham Printing. A few book printers exact a considerable fee for after-the-fact text changes, but not my favorite back-country printer.

The proofing process required several days time, interrupted by washing windows, weeding the flower beds, cooking, ironing, general household chores having a higher priority. But the thick pile of proofed pages were soon on their return journey to Gorham's.

Lesson #203. Get your "honey-do" jobs done before writing your first book.

A couple of days later, catching me with a half- sandwich in my mouth, Kurt called for a final once-over on the *Pete* book.

"Guess we're ready to roll," he said. "Just thought I'd call one last time to make sure we haven't forgotten anything. It's much easier to make changes now instead of after we've printed," he wisecracked.

"Ahe gugalod ouia weblot," I said.

"Huh?" Kurt questioned.

Gulp, I swallowed, then apologized, "Sorry, you caught me with a mouthful."

A couple of minor points had been under discussion. We quickly resolved those incidentals and I facetiously told Kurt, "Pete called this morning from up there and said he'd sue the pants off both of us if we put the picture of him with his big nose on the cover."

Kurt went along with the wittiness and shot back, "That's no problem, I'll put Kathy on it right now. She can shorten his nose. How long does he want it?"

"I didn't ask him but if she knocks about a foot off the length, that should please him."

Back to serious business, Kurt said, "We're ready to run, should have books for pickup by the end of next week."

"Sounds good, let me know when."

Me N' Pete was about to emerge as my first venture into the game of self-publishing.

Chapter 6

"Come 'n' get 'em," Kurt Gorham's voice invited over the phone. "Hey, Ron, we've got fourteen boxes of books here for you, hot off the press."

"I'll pick them up this afternoon," I replied, excited and jittery as a jaybird on a hot tin roof. After hanging up the phone I walked about six-inches above the floor, suspended in space, floating on my own dream cloud. At last, the long-awaited book that I'd only dared to visualize for the past five years had become a reality, an end result, the final stanza to the *Me N' Pete* friendship.

Gorham Printing will deliver books at no charge within sixty-miles of their print shop. Always eager, enthusiastic, and short on patience, I had to see the books as soon as they were available. Over the months Kurt had made a total of five pressruns of my two books. I picked up all five batches at his shop. The mileage became a deductible IRS expense, as well as an enjoyable drive in the country.

The weather gods had collaborated with the Chamber of Commerce on September 12, 1996 to generate as superb an autumn day as we'd ever enjoyed in the Pacific Northwest. Cloudless, warm but not stifling, just a hint of a southern breeze that rustled the arboreal canopy sheltering the woodsy country lane as I drove to the print shop. Windows down, I inhaled the plethora of outdoor aromas, nature's bouquet of blended fragrance. I sang a song to Cherokee only a tiny octave off-key, as we coursed the narrow byway through the tunnel-like trees. Yes, it was a magnificent day to be alive, to be alive amidst nature's grandeur.

Dusty's deep-toned *woof-woof* greeted me from the shop's porch. Kurt handed me a cup of coffee soon as I walked in.

"Black, or do I have to milk the cow?" he smiled.

"This is perfect, thanks."

"Did you bring the Jeep? It's getting like sardine-city in here. Sure would like to get rid of all fourteen cases."

"That shouldn't be any problem," I said, setting my cup down while opening one of the boxes. My eagerness to see the finished product had me on tenterhooks. I held the book up, studying it with rapt attention. There it was—*Me N' Pete,* just exactly like we'd planned it, just like I'd promised him that last day in the hospital that we'd do it, come hell or highwater.

Only authors would understand the feeling of exhilaration that swept over me as I held the book in my hands, at last a dream fulfilled. The pungent smell of the new ink, the stiffness of a never-before-opened book, the realization that I had brought all those jumbled words to a final creation.

"Well, how do you like it?" Kurt asked, leaning against an idle offset press while sipping his coffee and awaiting my reaction.

I brushed away a tear so he wouldn't notice. "Must be dusty in here," I mumbled as an explanation. "They look great to me. You and the gang did a tremendous job on my first venture into self-publishing."

"Shhh, not so loud," Kurt cautioned facetiously, "we don't want the troops to get overconfident."

But then he smiled a little hint of his pride in the work, and of his staff. "They do a good job and they know it," Kurt beamed.

Each gleaming white box, except for the last one, contained forty books and weighed something less than forty pounds. Kurt helped me load. I paid the second installment, shook hands with the boss and some of the "troops," and headed Cherokee down the lane.

I had scheduled the first two book-signings at two supermarkets to occur just one day after picking up the first printing at Gorham's. Close planning, but I had confidence that Kurt would have books ready when promised.

Going directly to the supermarkets from Gorham's, I left a full case (40) of books at each store. The clerks put a few books in the regular book section because the publicity had come out in that day's newspaper. They did sell a few copies of *Pete* even before the signing sessions.

In developing receipt forms I had obtained two-part, carbonless 8½x11 paper from our hometown printing company. A white, sensitive sheet was placed over a pink sheet. Writing on the white paper went through to the pink paper. I typed out a simple receipt form, blanks for store name, date, quantity of books, signature line, and typed them "three-up." (Three forms per 8½x11 white sheet.) I then copied the master form onto the white sheets which gave me three separate receipt forms per white page. Using a simple (39¢) dressmaker's serrated wheel, I scribed two horizontal perforations separating the three forms on the white sheet. Now stay with me on this!

In usage, the white sheet of three forms was placed atop the pink sheet. At my first store I filled out the bottom form of the three with store name, quantity of books delivered, date, and put an "X" on the signature line for the store's receiving employee to sign. Although there was no printing on the pink sheet, all writing on the white form, including signature, went through to the pink paper. When written I tore the white receipt at the perforation, leaving it with the store for their records. I had all the writing captured on the pink sheet for my own record. Each 8½x11 paper provided three receipt forms and worked o.k. so long as I remembered to fill out forms from the bottom (third) form up when placed on a clipboard.

I'm uncertain if the pink paper would copy and I really didn't care. If I'd copied the bottom (pink) sheet same as the white sheet, in usage the alignment would have to be perfect. With the writing going through to pink, it was easy to determine what store, on what date, received how many books, signed for by whom, no critical alignment required.

The form worked satisfactorily for all 5,700 books (five printings) we eventually distributed. The part I liked best was the cost, about six-cents for each receiving receipt.

If the description of my simple receipt form doesn't come through loud and clear, I invite anyone interested to mail me a SASE and I'll send you a facsimile of the form.

For money receipts I used the simple, off-the-shelf, 3¼x5½ two-part sales receipt pad. Each booklet contains fifty sets, a white top-copy with a carbon back on each sheet, and a duplicate yellow copy. Don't buy the booklet with just one sheet of carbon paper for the entire pad. You'll have to keep flipping the carbon each time.

I made these receipt forms on my word processor, three to a sheet, printed on the top copy of two part, pressure sensitive paper. They were separated by perforations made with a 39¢ dressmakers serrated wheel.

For under ten bucks I bought a push-down, customized ink stamp pad with my name, address and phone number, the kind that's spring-loaded and flips up when not in use. I stamped the top margin of each white sales slip which then became the customer's receipt. The yellow sheet stayed in the booklet for my record.

The cash receipt pads of fifty sets ranged in price from fifty-cents to a buck-fifty depending on where I bought them.

Guess how much old Scrooge paid for them? The price I didn't

77

This is a close-up look at the reciept from the previous page.

appreciate was the custom stamp pad, around nine dollars. I esti-mated I've used it about a thousand times (works great for stamp-ing envelope return addresses), so that's approximately a penny per impression. Another penny for each set of carbon receipts totals up to two-cents per money receipt written. The cost-each will dimin-ish as I continue using the stamp pad and amortize the initial cost.

Just one more expense before I was ready to sell books. I knew there was a need to publicize *Pete* in the stores with a half-way de-cent sign. Kinko's typeset a 11x17-inch master sign for me, listing title, what it was about, price, author's name, etc. The original type-setting was spendy—I think it cost me about fifteen bucks. Print-ing the actual signs myself from the master on colored card-stock was easy and inexpensive using Kinko's large copy machine. I re-call that each sign cost around twenty-cents. I needed to locate a friendly artist, or someone who could draw the master copy at little, if any expense. Maybe a free book in exchange? When I hand-painted them, my sign-making results resembled the art-work being done by elephant and chimpanzee zoo artists.

Lesson #204. Be frugal (cheap) with expenses.

Let's get out of this boring paperwork stuff and go sell books. That's where the money was—five bucks return for every seven-dollar book sold, net profit minus two dollars!

My deal with the supermarkets was simple and profitable—for them. I placed the books on consignment (as I did throughout the distribution of both books), only collected for books actually bought by the reading public. When sold, my cut was five-dollars for each $9.95 book sold. It's a good thing I'm not superstitious. The day of my first-ever book-signing dawned rainy, cold, windy, and—Friday the 13th. Quite a weather change from the previous day. I hoped it wasn't an omen.

A good friend, Al Calisewski (claims he's Irish), had retired from the wholesale grocery business as a broker's representative at the same time I retired. He, too, had been a good friend of Pete's. Without hobbies to keep him out of mischief, Al began accompanying me on book-selling, and signing trips. He was as enthusiastic about the *Pete* book as I was.

Coming from his broker's rep background, Al was about as timid as an aluminum siding salesman after a hurricane. Of medium height and weight, balding gray hair, often beaming his Polack smile, he talked endlessly, around-the-clock, but provided good company.

I was up and ready to go by eight a.m. Al had wanted to tag along, I think primarily to meet and talk with people. As I shaved and sipped my first of about ten cups of coffee that morning, I was excited, but also guardedly apprehensive. Would we sell books today? Would anyone show up for the signings?

It was about an hour's drive to the first customer-session at Pick-Rite Thriftway in Montesano. I parked at the far end of the rain-drenched supermarket parking lot, a courtesy habit developed during my wholesale grocery working career. Close parking was for customers—not sales people—especially in the rain.

Lesson #205. Don't park near a retailer's front door unless you're going in to spend some money with him.

"Jeez, are you going to make us walk a mile in this typhoon?"

Al asked.

"You sound like Pete," I replied. "That's what he would have said."

I pulled out of the distant parking spot, drove up to the market's front door and told Al, "There, is this better?" He got out, tucked a couple of my signs under his raincoat, and dashed through the downpour. I returned to the isolated parking spot and slogged the hundred yards back to the supermarket.

Montesano, less than 3,000 population, is the county seat of Grays Harbor County, the site of my growing up years, and also our own kids were raised there. I'd moved away twenty-five years earlier when my work dictated other locations. Being gone that long I wondered how many people I would recognize, or would recognize me.

As the market's automatic "In" door swung open, I shook water from my jacket and stomped it off my low-cut, dress oxfords. I glanced across the checkstands and noticed Al had already collared someone to talk with—Marc, the owner's son-in-law, and store manager. Soon I spotted Chris Pickering and his daughter, Ann, who welcomed me.

"I think you've got a couple of people waiting to buy your book," Chris said.

Marc had set up a table for me near the checkouts and had strewn the forty books I'd left in a helter-skelter pile atop the table.

Al had now switched his attention to a customer I didn't recognize who was holding one of my books in her hand. He was pointing out various pages in the book and giving her his very best sales pitch. This guy could sell raincoats in the Sahara on a hot day, any size, any color.

"Good morning, I'm Ron Fowler," I purred in my very best book-selling voice.

Al told her, "He's the guy who wrote this book. See, that's his picture on the back cover. Does he look like that?"

"Yes, I think it's a good resemblance. I'd like to buy one," the lady smiled. "Will you autograph it for me?"

I certainly will, no charge for autographs on Friday," I replied facetiously. "How may I personalize it for you?"

"Oh, you'll do that?" she questioned. "Well, I don't know. My name is Mary."

"How about, 'to Mary, have a good read,' and sign my name?"

"Yes, yes," she said, "that would be fine," reaching into her purse for her billfold.

"Oh, Mary," I advised, "we don't take the money. You'll pay at the checkstand along with any groceries you've bought."

She picked up the book, thanked both of us, and bee-lined for the first open checkstand.

In a few seconds, the cashier walked over to me, book in hand. "Your book won't scan," she said. (This meant the electronic reading head at the checkstand could not interpret the bar codes on the book.)

"Oh, maybe they haven't loaded it into the system," I replied. "To expedite the sale, it retails at $9.95. See the price on the back cover?"

This was my first skirmish with the bar code bollix. Early on, I assumed the supermarkets could load the code into their scanning system. Not so, I learned, supermarkets could not read bookstore bars, and vice versa.

We had no worry about selling books that day. During the first hour, ten to eleven o'clock, I was kept busy autographing without a break. At the peak of the rush we had as many as six people lined up, waiting patiently to buy a copy of *Pete*.

Al kept them entertained, moving in and out of the line, talking with any who would listen, and most did. Yada-yada-yada.

A cross-section of book-buyers showed up that morning: several former classmates I'd graduated from high school with 49-years ago; a couple of "shirttail" relatives on my former wife's side of the fence; some children of former friends (I'm Bill's son, you remember Bill?); a few oldtime business owners I barely recognized from 25-years past; and many people recently arrived whom I didn't know at all.

"I'll bet you don't recognize me," the next lady in line challenged.

"Well, Your face is familiar but I'm lost for putting a name on you," I apologized.

"We used to work at the newspaper together."

"Oh, sure, now I remember." I still wonder what her name was.

Just past eleven o'clock, Al shuffled up to my signing table where I'd just autographed another book. Walking slowly, hands extended like he was watching a dowsing rod, he carefully carried a foam cup of coffee. "Here," he said, "you'll need this shot of battery acid to recharge your cells. There's a coffee pot over in the bakery and it's free today for you and me. Boy, you've been pumping books out."

I'd noticed it had temporarily quit raining. "Thanks for the coffee. Why don't you take a shopping cart out to the Jeep and bring in another box of books," I suggested. "We only have a few left from the first box. Oh, and I'll need my clipboard with those perforated receipts too, Al."

"O.K., I'll need your keys," he said.

Although the rush of customers slowed a bit, there wasn't much down-time between signings during the remaining scheduled hour. One buyer was from Massachusetts—just passing through on vacation—happened to see the announcement of the signing.

Much of the credit for the substantial turnout of customers was due to the eye-catching advertisement the supermarket had published in the local weekly newspaper announcing the book-signing—the same newspaper I'd worked for 51-years previously.

The 2 column x 4-inch ad featured my picture, a little of my history, a synopsis of the book, and pertinent information regarding the signing. They had also done a feature article about me, but more importantly, about the book. This combination of publicity paid substantial dividends in customer turnout and book sales. Later, in a few locations where we didn't have newspaper publicity, we noticed fewer people turned out for the signings. I finally made a decision not to schedule signings/readings if media publicity was unavailable.

Lesson #206. Get publicity any legitimate way you can.

A few minutes before noon, Al and I began packing up signs and unsold books. It was a 20-minute drive to the next scheduled one o'clock market signing, plus we wanted to grab a quick lunch on the way.

As it happened, I sold about forty books at the first two-hour signing. I was quite certain the store would sell additional copies after the signing so we put ten *Pete* books on a spinner floor rack near the front checkstands.

Just prior to departing I cleared all my paperwork with Marc, the manager, thanking him for the splendid support. I also made arrangements to return in a couple of weeks to collect ($5.00) for each book sold.

While gobbling down a quick sandwich enroute to the Aberdeen supermarket, Al noted, "You did quite well for your first signing, forty sales in two hours."

"Yes, I'm really pleased with the way it went. I'm glad those forty people were interested enough to come down and buy a book. If they keep selling at this rate, we'll have a real vanilla day."

Chuck and Carl Swanson, long-time Aberdeen-Hoquiam (Washington) grocers, own three supermarkets in the twin seaport cities. Al, Pete and I had known the shrewd-operating brothers for almost fifty years. Chuck ran the grocery side of the markets; Carl's bailiwick was meat and produce. Al and I counted the brothers among our friends.

As we entered the Aberdeen store on that Friday afternoon, Chuck spotted us from his upstairs "crow's nest" office. "Well, here comes Ronnie and Calahoosky, we've been waiting for you peddlers. Let's sell some books!"

Many years ago Chuck had pinned us with those names and they stuck—at least for him. His eighty-plus years hadn't dampened his enthusiasm for the competitive grocery business on the "Harbor," or dimmed the darting twinkle in his narrowed Swedish eyes. Slightly stooped, wearing his usual James Cagney bill cap over his bald pate, he symbolized the patriarchy of down-home, sharp-witted businessmen.

Chuck had accompanied Pete and me on our Alaskan fishing trip, thus becoming a main character in one of my book's chapters:

"Pete's salmon was the only fish caught by either boat that first day. Back at the dock they weighed the monstrous fish at exactly 60-pounds.

"Well, it's dried out by now," Pete complained, "probably weighed about 80-pounds when I caught him."

Smiling, our fishing guide shook his head.

"Maybe 62-pounds, no more."

Back at camp that evening Pete couldn't resist the temptation to crow about his catch. Our foursome had established a money pot for the first, biggest, and most fish.

"I'm concerned about taking your money, and then deciding how to spend it," Pete joked.

"Looks like I'll win all three pots unless you guys get busy tomorrow."

Chuck said, "Pete, you caught the only fish today but this old Swede isn't through fishing yet."

On the following day Chuck reeled in a 68-pound salmon slab, taking our "biggest" pot and also walking off with the $500.00 weekly Soldotna town prize. Later that day he also boated a 53-pounder.

"Pete, now do you want to talk about who wins the "biggest," and "most" pots?" Chuck gloated.

"I never did care much for you damned Swedes," Pete replied, a feigned scowl on his face that quickly reverted to his trademark grin.

Back at the Aberdeen supermarket we walked past the store's hardware section. I smiled and called Al's attention to the monstrous, mounted king salmon displayed on the wall. "That's Chuck's big prize-winner from Alaska," I explained.

As our last store had done, Swanson's had set up a signing table complete with chairs near the front checkstands. The *Pete* books I'd delivered the previous day were displayed on the table along with a copy of the ad they had run about the book in the local newspaper.

Several potential customers milled around the book table, flipping pages. "Guess I'd better get to work, can I sign a book for anybody here?" I asked, sidling up to the table.

A middle-aged lady handed me the book she had been looking at, "Yes, I want one. I knew Pete quite well when he used to come to Grayland."

"I remember he talked about Grayland often, in fact he stayed in a motel over there," I said.

"Yes, he did, cabin number four," she replied matter-of-factly.

I decided to let the conversation end there before she told me things I might not want to know.

The second signing session went much like the first with continuous customers during the opening hour. Again, some old friends; a couple of former classmates; surprisingly, our physician who had treated us and our munchkins when we lived in Montesano; one of my favorite cousins who I hadn't seen for 25-years.

Several people, many I did not know, bought more than one book, probably for a birthday or Christmas present.

I had thought Chuck Swanson was rather lukewarm to the *Pete* book considering that his picture with the 68-pound salmon was in the Alaska chapter. He seemed to mask his indifference with an attitude of detachment. I had inquired, "Have you had a chance to read the book yet?" He shook his head, "no."

Any thought of nonchalance was dispelled when he called me up to his office during the final hour of my signing. Pulling a crumpled list of names from his pocket, he timidly said, "Ronnie, here is a list of names I'd like you to personalize with your book, then sign your name and the date. Helen (Chuck's wife), and I are going to give them as presents."

I was pleasantly surprised by his action, and it indicated I was mistaken about his indifference. He truly was pleased with being the featured salmon fisherman, especially being the prize-winning fisherman. He bought eleven books for gift-giving. Later, I realized the old, gray fox was getting $9.95 presents, author-autographed at five bucks each, or half-price. But, I was glad to have the business.

Al and I closed up shop at four o'clock, having had to bring in two more boxes from our reserve stock. I felt satisfied with the two signings, and the number of books we'd sold.

Heading down the freeway for home in the late afternoon traffic, I told Al, "We had a good day. According to my mental math, we sold 93 books during the two signings."

"Just proves what I've always heard," Al replied. "Publish it and they will come."

Chapter 7

During the remainder of 1996 I diligently worked at selling my *Pete* book whenever, wherever, and however possible.

Following the two initial book-signings at the supermarkets, Kit and I had volunteered for another out-of-country I.E.S.C. project. On September 28th we flew to Monterrey, Mexico for our second visit to that sprawling city of four-million inhabitants. Two years earlier we had worked with a different Mexican grocery wholesaler. Upon return to the good ol' U.S., our tortured bodies required a few days of R & R in Palm Springs, acclimatizing ourselves back into a more familiar culture and environment. We were glad to be home on November 13th.

Life was crazy for the next few months, absolutely crazy, but, in some ambiguous way, it was personally rewarding. I peddled the *Pete* book, continued writing, *Rubles For Wodka*, researched and interviewed for my John Tornow book, while setting up *Pete* distribution through two new distributors.

In December Al and I went back to Grays Harbor for more *Pete* book-signings. I scheduled sessions again at all three of Swanson's supermarkets, and also took another shot at Pick-Rite in Montesano. I told Al that people should give *Pete* for Christmas even if their friends and relatives wouldn't read it. The book makes a festive holiday doorstop.

We banged out three, two-hour signings at Swanson's in one day, December 12th, selling a total of 71 books. Several direct sales resulted from word-of-mouth advertising as people mailed checks, or called to have me send books via U.S. mail.

I no longer agonized about having unsold books on my hands from the *Pete* printing. Noting how well the book was selling, I was "whelmed," but not quite "overwhelmed."

During the signing session at Swanson's a tall, gangly fellow came over and introduced himself. He looked like a basketball center, a college professor and a used car salesman all rolled into one body.

"Hi, my name's Dick Moulton, former county extension agent now dabbling in book distribution. I wished we'd gotten together before your signings. I would have liked to have been able to distribute your book."

That's really heaven-sent, I thought to myself. Just what I need, another middleman to take a couple more bucks off the proceeds of the *Pete* book, and put me even deeper in the hole.

Recognizing that honesty probably bankrupted more than one struggling self-publisher, nonetheless I laid my cards on the table with Moulton.

"This book is somewhat of a monetary fiasco for me. I'm wholesaling it at five-dollars after the printing cost was seven, and that doesn't include a whole passel of extracurricular expenses."

Moulton flashed a hesitant, understanding smile, his eyebrows arched like bristly half-moons, "None of us get rich in this book business, but it sounds like you're getting even less rich. I'm presently servicing Swanson's and some 30-plus other stores with a line of historical and inspirational books. I could easily absorb your book into my lineup, and would be willing to pay your five-dollar wholesale cost even though it would necessitate a price increase on your book to Swanson's and Pick-Rite. I think they would understand that they will be paying a pittance for my service," he concluded.

I found out later there are usually independent book distributors located around the country who are anxious to take on distribution of short-run volumes. These entrepreneurs are often the answer for small self-publishers to obtain limited distribution of their books. The best way to locate them is to ask lower volume retail outlets where they buy their books.

I mustered sufficient courage one day to break the news at Swanson's.

"Chuck, we've probably already enjoyed most of the sales we're going to get on my *Pete* book. Your three stores have sold almost two-hundred and I think that's quite an achievement. If it's alright with you, Dick Moulton has offered to take over servicing my book along with the others you buy from him. I'll still drop in to say 'hello' once in awhile, but not to sell books."

"Sure, that will be fine, Ronnie, but we'll miss seeing you as often. Will the price to us increase on the *Pete* book?"

I knew price would be a major consideration and an important hurdle we'd need to cross in order to make the transition. "I'm uncertain what Dick's pricing policy is. Being one of his largest customers you must be getting the most favorable discount he offers. But in all honesty, there probably will be an increase. I've been selling them to you at about forty-percent off retail. I think Dick's price will be slightly higher."

Chuck's countenance now reflected his more somber, businesslike look. "We'll give it a try, and if the price goes up too much, we'll yell at you guys for a better deal," he concluded. I scheduled a meeting with Dick Moulton in his office-away-from-office at the ever-popular Bee Hive Restaurant in Montesano. From there he counseled wannabe agronomists in the art of soil science, while hawking his latest literary offerings.

"You'll need to count the number of *Pete* books in each store," I said, "as of that day, I'll invoice the stores for the total number of books I've delivered to them, less the ones you've inventoried. I'll move those quantities over to your account. You can pay me on thirty-day terms."

"That's cool!" Gray-haired Grandpa Dick said. I suppose he picked *that* up from his grandkids. "I'll probably need a box of *Pete* books to sell to my other accounts."

At that time Dick and I entered into a gentleman's agreement not to infringe on each other's territory. It was necessary because we each had a different pricing structure for our retail accounts. Throwing two diverse discounts at the same customer could cause as much uneasiness as receiving an "Urgent" letter from the I.R.S.

On the boundary of the territories, we reached a mutually satisfactory agreement on who took responsibility for certain retailers. Throughout both distributions of books, our agreement worked well for us. So well that, on several occasions, I would check inventories at some of Dick's customers. If they needed books, I would leave them from my car-stock, get a signed receipt, and mail it to Dick so he could collect for the books I'd left them. I then added the quantity against Dick's account.

Many times when Dick needed inventory and our paths were not going to cross, I dropped off books valued at several hundred dollars with one of "my retailers" for him to pick up. No paperwork, no signatures, just good old down-home trust. It was good for both of us.

Around that time I continued writing the *Rubles For Wodka* book about our Russian experiences. Once again I flooded the literary pipelines with query letters, trying to get at least a "maybe" from a literary agent, or publisher. However, in Russian words, all I heard was, "Nyeht."

Discouraged by a lack of positive feedback, my attention switched focus to my third book project. From my early newspaper days at the Montesano Vidette, the controversial story of Northwest outlaw, John Tornow had always fascinated me. I had researched and interviewed people in the mid-1940's who had known the Tornow family in the early 1900's; pioneers from the backwoods timber-country like Albert Kuhnle; city residents, like Ora Watson, who had deer-hunted with John.

There had been dozens of short stories about Tornow, each with a different twist, each with a contradictory opinion about whether he was guilty of the original crime charged to him. In all of my research, I could not find that anyone had ever written a full-length book about John Tornow.

Why not? If the story fascinated me, why wouldn't it be interesting to the general public? The saga contained mystery and intrigue; the story was a significant slice of Northwest history; there was a depiction of the internal strife that developed between two early homestead families; the story's setting was in the beautiful Olympic Mountain foothills; and last, it provided insight into the psychological turmoil within the mind of a slightly demented person, and also questioned whether John Tornow was born with normal human qualities?

Considering the marketability and feasibility of a John Tornow book became an exciting subject to embroil my cerebral nogginoids. I felt the book would be popular in our local region, but I was uncertain (and still am) how it would be received in general distribution.

While selling *Pete* with one hand, the other mitt began digging up all the research material I had collected about the enigmatic Northwest outlaw. I had even written a few preliminary chapters in earlier years.

Kit and I visited the original Tornow homestead in 1994 and spent an enjoyable couple of hours with Mrs. Bud Larson, who, along with her husband, now own the tidy little farm where the early homesteaders first tilled the Satsop valley soil.

Mrs. Larson showed us the original log cabin built by Fritz Tornow in the late 1800's. We were amazed that the cabin was in such good condition for its years. The Tornow parents, Fritz and Louisa, raised six children in the tiny 16x20 abode before constructing a larger wooden frame house on the front of the property. It would have been a feat in itself to squeeze six kids and two adults into the tiny cracker-box cabin. The Larsons have removed one end of the original log home and have converted it into a one-car garage. Small scraps of newspaper can still be found on interior log walls, pasted there by the family for insulation.

On this same day, Kit and I stopped at the small Grove Cemetery, a community place of interment for some deceased pioneer Matlock residents. Located in a peaceful, tree-lined setting a few miles north of the homestead, we found John Tornow's grave as well as his parents. Three children of Minnie Tornow Bauer, John, William, and Mary, each of whom had a tragic role in the Tornow episode are also interred in the rural cemetery which lies alongside the Brady-Matlock asphalt highway.

Continuing northward, Kit and I soon came to the Mary M. Knight school where the local volunteer historical society has established a museum in a pioneer home on the south end of the schoolgrounds. The museum contains a most complete collection of Tornow memorabilia, plus many early historical and pioneer artifacts from the surrounding area. Not the Smithsonian, but the dedicated volunteers have managed to preserve much of the past in this rustic old house.

I had begun writing a few chapters of the John Tornow book several years prior to *Pete*. Tornow's parents had immigrated from Germany so I decided to develop their dialogue using the German speech inflection as I had thought it would sound in their daily conversations. In that vernacular, "w" became "v", "t" sounded like "d", "j" was "y", etc. A typical sentence, "Well Mother, we should boil the water," becomes, "Vel Mudder, ve should boil der vater."

I expended considerable time and effort to translate each spoken sentence into the Mother-tongue, a real enigma of elucidation. Slowly, sentences developed into paragraphs, those even slower, like a glacier's uphill pace, became pages, which in turn formed overdue chapters. I was as pleased as a "hawg" cruising seventy down an open highway when I'd completed all the translations. The dialogue looked good to me until a knowledgeable reviewer read it.

"What's this spelling?" he asked.

"That reflects the guttural elucidation of the German language," I beamed, so satisfied was I with my attempt to make the dialogue sound realistic to the character's country of origin.

"Not good," he replied. "That's not good at all. As an interested reader of your book it makes me slow down, stumble, then stop while my eyes tell my brain what they see. You never want this to happen, never want to slow down, or stop a reader. The dialogue should flow smoothly. If it doesn't, the reader will become irritated at having to stop frequently trying to decipher what the next word is. It's o.k. to use colloquial idioms as long as they're done in English, like; 'Fancy meeting you here, or I was just getting forty winks,' but stay away from, 'mudder and fahder.'"

Tossing those chapters into the round file like they'd just been slam-dunked by Michael Jordan, I thought, vell dere goes a couple more weeks of wasted vernacular ingenuity.

Lesson #207. Don't muddy-up the English language anymore than it already is.

Jumping forth and back between writing/researching my John Tornow book, *Guilty By Circumstance* which we will henceforth shorten to *Tornow*, and selling *Pete* which you'll remember is *Me N' Pete*, I tried to establish an acceptable balance between the two. Surprisingly, our Basin, Wyoming program with Barnes and Noble chugged along satisfactorily on the *Pete* book. Their three close stores ordered books which I delivered, then mailed the paperwork to Charley Soames. At least I'd thought it was chugging along, even though I hadn't seen the color of the ink on Charley's checks, and didn't until we were sixty-days into the program.

I had scheduled firm reading/signing dates with two of the B & N, Community Relations Coordinators. The third store wanted to wait and see how successful the other two went. That puckered me a bit—her not scheduling—but I went along.

Mary, the perky local B & N, C.R.C. ordered 25 books from me, predicated on the scheduled reading/signing, plus my hometown author claim to fame. The other two stores ordered just eight books each (the cowards!). I wasn't concerned about the quantities, because with Charley's program, I could deliver books to them everyday if necessary. Only problem was the wear and tear on Cherokee. Also, the stores knew I was guaranteeing the sale, so they could return any unsold *Petes*.

A week prior to the first signing I had ever done with B & N, I went to the local store to check with Mary, the C.R.C., to make certain we were coordinated. As I walked in, I was greeted by a 22x28 inch professional poster sign: "Barnes & Noble welcomes Ron Fowler, author of *Me N' Pete*, discussion and book signing on..." Seeing that sign made this greenhorn author feel pretty darned good.

"Hi, Mary, are we all set for next Saturday's signing?" I asked.

With a broad smile, bubbling like a tea kettle with enthusiasm, she said, "We're ready if you are. Let's see, we've already sold a couple of your books from our 'Local Author' display table. If we need more than the twenty-three I have, you'll have backup stock, won't you?"

I assured her I would have more books if needed. She showed me the area of the store where they setup the lectern, signing table, and about twenty chairs for the anticipated audience. B & N issues a monthly newsletter in-house where they had listed and explained my event. Also, the week of the signing, a separate flyer for each in-house event, with author's name, picture, book title, day and time is given out to each customer at the store. Normally, B & N lists their events in a regular column in the local newspaper, but

These high-quality posters were prominently displayed in Barnes & Noble bookstores to announce upcoming book signings and readings. The signs were very legible and eye-catching, providing good attendance at most events.

some glitch prevented mine from appearing. As I mentioned earlier, B & N does a splendid job of in-house promotion; not as well with the outside general public news sources.

Although the one B & N, C.R.C. didn't want to schedule my event, in most cases, the coordinators emphasized author events. It almost seemed like a competition where one store would vie with others for the most events. I had received requests from distant C.R.C's wanting to put me on their event schedules. I complied with the stores I thought would have a chance to sell any of my books.

A bluebird spring afternoon augured well for my long-awaited first appearance at Barnes & Noble. I dressed my best, polished my notes (as well as my shoes) for the thirty-minute reading, loaded an extra box of forty books aboard Cherokee, left home a half-hour early for a ten-minute drive to the local B & N.

What a glorious day for my first bookstore appearance, I told Cherokee! It was so warm I left my jacket in the Jeep. Not many people around the mall for a Saturday afternoon, I noted.

Mary saw me come in, fifteen minutes early. "I'm a bit worried," she said, a frown furrowing her normally unruffled brow. "Business has been slow today, much unlike a normal Saturday. My concern, this is the first warm day we've had this spring, and I think people are staying home to work in their yards. Maybe we should have scheduled you during an evening," she said.

I tried to look calm and assured, hiding the pain of the ninety-pound concrete block that her comments had caused to hit my stomach and bounce up into my throat.

"Well, they will probably drift in a little later," I said, knowing full well I was lying between my teeth.

Looking around the bookstore, I only saw three or four people. One of those was an elderly gentleman fast asleep in one of the comfortable upholstered chairs. A mother led her young daughter towards the children's book section. A youngish looking couple studied maps in the travel section, probably planning a trip. No *Pete* book buyers there.

I returned to my lectern, intently studied my notes to appear busy, and closed my eyes to the sea of empty chairs that seemed to stare blankly at the guest author. A middle-aged lady came through the front door, caught my eye and headed in my direction. Aha, I rejoiced, my first customer. At the last instant, her high heels clicking like castanets, she veered off down the biography aisle.

An hour into the schedule, Mary came over to my deserted area.

"Kind of slow, huh?" she said.

"Yes, but it's early," I theorized.

"If you'd like a cup of coffee, Barnes & Noble buys for all guest authors on our programs," she said, valiantly trying to shore up her now wavering, exuberant disposition.

"The way it's going, you won't make enough profit from my sales today to pay for a cup of coffee."

"That's o.k.," she shrugged, "it all averages out."

Just before the end of my scheduled time, a well-dressed young man sauntered over to my table where I had displayed all B & N's twenty-three copies. He picked one up, flipped the pages but stopped to look at pictures. I immediately launched into my sales pitch explaining what the book was about. I felt like I'd "hooked" a customer and wasn't about to let him get away. If I'd had a net, I would have popped it over his head.

The young man put the book down and I thought for just an instant he was reaching for his wallet. Instead, he just hitched his trousers up a notch, casually walked away, uttering just one word. "Interesting," he said.

Lesson #208. Don't sniffle if you build it and they don't come.

And that's how my first ever Barnes & Noble book-signing fell flat as unsalted popcorn. Not a single customer, not even one sale. I was devastated and very embarrassed. Remember earlier I had mentioned that being an author required having the thick skin of a Rhodesian rhinoceros. However, this wasn't the only astonishing setback we encountered in this crazy, unpredictable book selling game. Why? There was no rationale to explain the "iffiness" of the book buying public. We'd sold 71 books at the grocery supermarkets, but none, zero, zilch, at the bookstore signing.

During the ensuing months, both Al and I were altogether astounded by the unpredictability, even from location to location, week to week. One retail store sold out in a week, but across the street and two blocks away, not a single sale.

Then, the first hot location sold none in a month, while the second store ran out of books in a matter of days. We finally learned to just shrug it off, not even try to explain the topsy-turvy scenario that plagued the business of selling books.

My second B & N reading/signing session in Olympia, Washington State's capital city, was scheduled during evening hours and was better attended. About half the twenty-some attendees were friends and acquaintances. I'd organized a thirty-minute talk about the book, self-publishing, and a few humorous incidents encountered along the literary trail. A lively Q & A session followed my remarks, and demonstrated there was considerable interest in writing books and self-publishing. We also sold about a dozen copies of *Pete*. The session did wonders for my drooping ego and slumping self-confidence.

* * *

In early 1997 I'd made arrangements with Rand Iversen, President of the M.M.K. historical program to visit and spend research time at the seldom-open museum on the schoolgrounds near Matlock. I felt their Tornow documents and memorabilia would help corroborate, perhaps even expand, on the material I had collected down through the years. I wanted to be as factual as possible after 85 years of so-called eyewitness reports, third-hand hearsay, and exaggerated John Tornow legends. Before documenting an incident as factual, I tried to obtain at least two corroborating statements from qualified sources. Even then, if a story

In the John Tornow section of the Matlock Historical Museum, Rand Iversen, Dr. John Tornow and the author discuss the remarkable story of outlaw John Tornow.

didn't seem plausible, I discarded it.

One example of an oft-told Tornow tale described how the forest outlaw tied frogs with elk hair. He eluded posses sent out to capture him in the rugged foothills of Washington's Olympic Mountains for nineteen months. Posses finally located him at a remote alpine lake. Tornow's camp was adjacent to a marshy bog inhabited by a large family of frogs. Instinctively, croaking frogs will shush if they sense the approach of man or beast. The cunning outlaw used this wilderness security alarm system to his advantage. But there was no need to tie the green, hippity-hoppers. They lived there. Secondly, I could not envision Tornow struggling with a squiggly frog in an attempt to tie it with a slick, narrow, six-inch long elk hair. Tie to what? Popular legend dismissed as being unbelievable.

Lesson #209. If it seems impossible, it probably is.

While at the M.M.K. Museum, I noted they had several pictures pertaining to the Tornow saga that I didn't have. Looking ahead to the day my *Tornow* book would be printed, I asked Rand Iversen if I could borrow the pics to have copies made. It was obvious he was concerned about losing the irreplaceable prints. At that time, Rand didn't know me from a hemlock stump, so I couldn't blame his reluctance. I promised him I would use a familiar, nearby (Shelton WA) photo studio to make the duplicates, and this seemed to allay his concerns.

Spearheaded by Rand Iversen, a John Tornow forum had been held in the M.M.K. school gymnasium in the spring of 1995.

Several authors, including myself, who were known to have been writing about the forest outlaw, were invited to attend and discuss the story.

"Downtown Matlock" consists of a general store/ post office with sparsely-populated farms and forest dwellings scattered within a five-mile radius. Realizing it wasn't a bustling metropolis, I was amazed to see the SRO crowd of more than two-hundred people who turned out for the forum. I think that was indicative of the interest generated by the Tornow chronicle. I was not surprised, however, to hear widely differing versions of the story from each author who spoke at the forum. I mention this meeting in order to explain how I obtained what I consider to be the most noteworthy picture in the entire collection. At the end of the forum, a Tornow afficionado, Ted Rakoski, presented a framed picture of the entire Tornow family posed against the side of the still-standing log cabin. I don't believe any of us even knew the print existed, but be assured I tracked down Mr. Rakoski and obtained a copy of this prized find for my collection.

One last chuckle on this incident, I gave Rakoski a credit line for the picture as used in the *Tornow* book. Only problem was, I misspelled his name. A few days after distributing the first printing, I received a scathing letter in the mail from Mr. Rakoski (correct spelling), telling me what he thought of authors who didn't take the time to verify names. The oversight was corrected in the second, and subsequent printings. I sent Rakoski a gratis book containing the correct spelling, and humbled myself for his forgiveness.

Lesson #210. Exercise caution when spelling names.

Chapter 8

The *Pete* book was selling well through bookstore and supermarket events, but I still had a couple hundred copies stacked up in my office in early 1997. This was about the time I made a rather lamebrained mistake which I'll share with you.

I'm a hardened, habitual worrier. Not the common, garden variety type, rather a worrier who, when everything is coming up champion, I worry I soon might not have anything to worry about. At that time, having little to stew over, I decided to target-worry those unsold books.

Scanning through a national hunting-fishing magazine one day while plucking my eyebrows between thumb and forefinger, I noticed the mag was running a half-price special on their classified advertising. The hype went something like: "This month only, fifty-percent discount on all classified advertising, call Mr. So-and-So to place your ad." My normally lethargic noggin-wheels came to life as I fell into a mode of calculation. This magazine must be read by millions, well maybe at least thousands, of enthusiastic outdoor people who would pay great sums of cash money to read my hilariously humorous *Pete* book.

With only weeks remaining before the deadline, I sat down and scribbled a classified ad for their "Outdoor Books" column, then called Mr. S-and-S. They charged by the letter, or word, so I didn't get rambly, also utilized abbreviations wherever possible. It read: "*Me N' Pete*, a 256-page true, humorous hunt-fish experiences in Pac-Nor'west. Send $12 incl. p & h to..." I fidgeted for an eternity before it appeared in print, at which time I just sat back, hands folded behind head, waited for the avalanche of mail-orders to roll in. I worried maybe our little post office couldn't handle such an influx of new mail. Was our mailbox big enough to contain the daily surge?

One week plodded past. Then another. I began to worry—no mail-orders. The third week I finally did receive a letter. It was from the hunting-fishing magazine, an invoice, said I owed them $63.25 for the ad. To this day I never received a single order from that advertisement. I had even included a line in the ad, "Money-back guarantee." It would have been nice if the magazine had provided that same offer.

Lesson #211. Only legendary Rumplestiltskin could weave a golden book cover from a ho-hum classified ad.

Despite my anxiety about sales, the *Pete* book continued to move out of my inventory—a few more signings; sales through Dick Moulton; Charley Soames; and one-sy, two-sy word of mouth sales.

In March, a regional book reviewer under the name of "Bookmonger," to whom I had sent a copy of Pete, gave my book a more-or-less favorable review in local daily newspapers. I was quite appreciative of *any* mention she made, but for her to be somewhat congratulatory really made my day. I quote excerpts from her column appearing in the *Tacoma News Tribune*, and other metropolitan papers:

> "Self-publishing and subsidy publishing generally don't enjoy much cachet, but *Me N' Pete* is seeing the light of day because the author invested his own resources in getting the book to press."
>
> "As set down in this book, the friends' mishaps and ad-

ventures in the great outdoors are moderately entertaining, but what Fowler does best is recreate the lively camaraderie that sparked between his buddy and him—the quips fairly crackle across the pages."

In retrospect, I believe the "Bookmonger's" review was more laudatory than I deserved—but, what the heck, I'll accept praise, even—"moderately entertaining"—anytime, anywhere.

Recognizing the *Pete* book would soon be sold out, I intensified my writing/research of the John Tornow saga. I visited every conceivable source of historical data in the state, gathering bits and pieces along the way. Numerous library archives provided written articles, interviews and newspaper news stories about the outlaw during the early days of his escapades. My appetite for Tornow tips became insatiable. I relied heavily on the personal interviews I had done in the mid-1940's with reliable people who provided earwitness accounts of happenings during the era.

Separating truth from fiction became a major undertaking. I felt like a twentieth-century Diogenes, shining my light throughout the woods of the Northwest in search of an honest man with unexaggerated Tornow information. And some did exaggerate.

I interviewed one pundit who claimed to be an authority on the Northwest outlaw. I remember him from the stained woolen sweater he wore that gave no indication, coloring or cleanliness, that anything had been done to the material since it had been separated from the sheep. I had to bite my lip to restrain my urge to laugh hysterically at his revelations.

"Do you know how John was able to stay alive for nineteen months while the Sheriff chased him?" the sage queried.

"Well, my research indicates he lived off the land and occasionally visited a farmer's garden or root cellar."

"That ain't all," my informant related. "He had a friend in Seattle."

"A friend in Seattle?" I asked incredulously.

"Yep," he said, flashing a smirk of flawed wisdom. "The friend owned a grocery store and supplied John with grub."

"But Seattle is ninety-miles from Matlock."

"Don't matter none. John was tough. He walked it. And that ain't all, you know why the Sheriff could never find none of Tornow's tracks?"

"The old-timers seemed to think he knew the woods and only walked where his tracks wouldn't show," I replied, searching for a quick exit from the sparkling conversation.

"Nope, he lived in the trees."

"Lived in the trees?" Repeating his words to make sure my hearing hadn't failed me.

"Yep, and when he wanted to go somewheres he just swung from tree to tree like Tarzan."

"Like Tarzan?" I again repeated. His speculative announcement had me mesmerized.

"In fact," the gentleman continued, "Tornow gave Edgar Rice Burroughs the idea for his Tarzan character."

That did it, I needed to escape. "Sorry, I've got to go, I'll be late for my streetcar."

"Streetcar?" I heard him mumble as I made tracks, "There ain't no streetcars around here."

While continuing to write the *Tornow* book, I bombarded publishers and agents again with queries to determine interest in the outlaw's story. Shades of the *Pete* experience—no takers. I felt astonished and somewhat discouraged, astonished because I knew the Tornow story contained all elements necessary for a successful book. But there didn't seem to be a publisher within range of the U.S. Postal Service who agreed with me. My greatest dilemma was trying to determine if the subject was uninteresting, or if the quality of my writing was earning me all those turndowns. I knew I had to remain steadfast, knew the Tornow story would sell if only

I had sufficient talent to wordsmith it satisfactorily. I resisted the inclination to allow the wet-blanket refusals to douse my pilot light of exuberance.

Just about this time, with rejection notices from publishers piled much higher than my enthusiasm, I think, in a half-hearted manner I accepted the probability it would be difficult—if not impossible—to find an interested publisher. At this point, *Tornow* had self-publish written all over it. Thinking of such a monumental task reminded me of the monetary debacle I experienced on the *Pete* book. Our bank account would challenge the national debt if forced to endure another incomeless publishing ordeal. Besides, I had no desire to subject my slumberland body to the rigors of the sofa springs at Kit's direction.

Another quashing straw on the literary camel's back came in the form of a surprising announcement. When I'd almost run out of *Pete* books, Charley, my Wyoming distributor ran out on me. A notice arrived in the mail that Wolverine Distributing would no longer be selling books to Barnes & Noble. This had minimal impact on *Pete* because my inventory was down to less than fifty books. But it concerned me how I could get my smallfry foot in the door with the national booksellers if, and when, I self-published *Tornow*. The main players, Borders, B & N, Walden, Crown, required placement through an authorized distributor—a function capably performed by Charley in the past, albeit at a lowered author profit-level. Without the middleman, self-publishing would become increasingly more difficult.

Within a matter of weeks, the distribution problem, as it effected me anyway, was resolved. A major book distributor, at least major in our neck of the woods, announced they were closing their doors. Before the second shoe could drop, "Partners," another significant book distributor announced they would soon open a warehouse in Seattle, "Partners West." They were an approved supplier for most national booksellers, and within easy driving distance from my home. I often wondered what, if any, impact these events might have had on Wolverine's decision.

Nonetheless, in June, 1997, Kit and I attended my 50th high school graduation reunion in Montesano. The celebration was held at the same location the Playhouse Tavern had occupied, operated by Mom and Dad, fifty-three years earlier. Thinking back on all the beer that had flowed out of the barrels, I didn't feel one bit older than my 106-years. From a class of 48 graduates, 13 were deceased, 26 attended the reunion. During my master-of-ceremonies duty at the gala, I also sold twelve *Pete* books to former classmates.

Lesson #212. Even when you're 106-years old, sell, sell, sell.

Whether I was fortunate enough to land a paying publisher, or self-published Tornow, I would have to enlarge my collection of usable photos. My minimum target was to have twenty printed pictures, necessitating a collection of around thirty to choose from. We eventually printed 24-pics, including the cover photo.

I called Al one late spring day in '97. "What have you got planned for tomorrow?"

"Just watching TV and my afternoon nap," he replied with a yawn. "Why, whatcha got cookin?'"

"I need to go to Matlock and take a few pictures. Do you want to go along? You can take your nap on the trip home."

The drive up the beautiful Satsop River valley on that warm June morning made us appreciate our good fortune of living in such a magnificent outdoors. Bathed in warm sunshine, robins hunted worms in the low fields where the evening's dew had evaporated and the countryside appeared to have fully renewed its glorious coloring.

Al summed it up. "They call this God's country, and I'll bet if He had to pick a spot, He'd live on one of these 80-acre rolling farms alongside the river."

The country lane wandered through lush green pasturelands bordered with woodlands of arrow-straight Douglas fir trees, nearly as tall as the sky. Through it all flowed the clear bubbling Satsop river, it's waters rushing from the towering Olympic Mountains and cascading to the blue Pacific Ocean. Symbolic Shangri-la.

Our first stop was at the Matlock General Store where we talked with Jim and Laurie, young husband-wife team who enjoy the friendships of the locals, but still derive satisfaction from their laid-back isolation.

Quite familiar with the Tornow episode, Jim said, "If your book is ever published, we want to sell it out here. Sometimes John Tornow is about the only subject we've got to talk about."

I photographed the store at its crossroads location in "downtown Matlock." In the heyday of the Tornow era, the village included more than a dozen various businesses. Today, the General Store is Matlock.

We passed by the Mary M. Knight school and museum where I had already taken pictures, then continued a couple miles to the tiny Grove Cemetery. It was eerily quiet and deserted, a bit spooky. Strolling over to John Tornow's grave, we were surprised to find two shotgun shells, a few .22 cartridges and twenty-four cents in coins.

"People must leave these things in John's memory," Al remarked with a grin. Nearby we found three empty beer cans—Miller High Life.

The polarized sun was good for a picture of John's headstone, so I snapped several. Al and I resisted the temptation to remove any of the memorabilia. It's bad luck, you know.

We turned up the West Boundary Road to the former homestead of Henry Bauer and his wife, Minnie, John Tornow's sister. Here again, the first buildings, dating back to the 1880's, still stand. The original tiny cabin where the Bauers raised three offspring is situated behind the larger home with it's curlicue gingerbread trim and real glass windows. More photos.

Just down the road a piece, Mrs. Bud Larson gave us the run of the former Tornow homestead when I explained we wanted to photograph the original log cabin the family patriarch had built in the 1880's.

"Just knock on the door if you have any questions," the genial farm-wife said. I finished my roll of film, snapping pictures inside and outside the log cabin.

Pulling back onto the blacktop highway, I told Al, "Now you can take an hour's nap before we get back to civilization."

"I'd rather stay awake and talk to you," he said.

An unlimited vocabularist, talk he did.

The photo finisher had the pictures back in less than a week— enough time for me to receive three more *Pete* rejection notices. I laid out all the prints pertaining to the *Tornow* book, including several unpleasant pictures of John after he'd been shot. I was looking for a print suitable for the book's cover—it had to be a good one— appropriate, not gory—but indicative of the story. My eyes roamed the montage searching for the perfect cover shot. Then I saw it—the tombstone—why not?

For seventy-four years the only marker on John's grave had been a small piece of concrete, simply inscribed "J.T." We had assumed the family feared grave desecration if it had been prominently identified.

In 1987 a monument company designed and constructed a very appropriate and attractive headstone. Below John's name is: "SEPT. 4, 1880—APRIL 16, 1913," the years of his life. The inscription reads: "FROM LONER—TO OUTCAST—TO FUGITIVE." Again, very appropriate. Below that, the artist had carved a scene onto the three-foot tall slab of Northwest granite depicting the Bauer twins on a bear-hunting expedition. This was the tragic incident that ignited the nineteen-month manhunt for John Tornow. I was elated to have found the perfect cover photo.

Although I doubted it was necessary to obtain permission, I phoned the monument builder.

"I'm Ron Fowler and I've written a book on the life of John Tornow. I like the headstone you've installed on his grave and plan to use a picture of it on the cover of my book."

Over the phone I heard a hesitant chuckle. "Oh, you are, huh?" he said, more of a statement than a question. "Will your publisher have an artist on staff?"

This seemed like a strange inquiry, I paused before replying, "Well...yes...I guess so. Why do you ask?"

"Do you have a picture of the headstone in front of you right now?"

"Yes," I answered, retrieving it from the pile of prints I planned for the book.

The artist said, "Look at the word, 'fugitive.'"

"Oh, my God!" I'd looked at that headstone a dozen times, photographed it several times, but never noticed the error. He had spelled the word, "Fugitive," F-U-G-I-T-V-E, leaving out the second "i." Talk about having something carved in stone!

"Yes, I see what you mean. I think that can be corrected," I assured him.

"It would be greatly appreciated," the erring stonecutter replied.

Lesson #213. Buy a good dictionary before carving in stone.

I had written most of the book's dialogue in the first person, trying to duplicate what I thought the non-fictional characters would have said in the various true-to-life circumstances. I had been told this fabrication alone would preclude the book's genre being categorized as non-fiction. Everything I had written was as factual as my research would provide, so it disturbed me not to have the classification of non-fiction.

One day, my editor, Mary Ryan, the tough critic, told me, "Ron, the

A physician relocating to the Tacoma area browsed a Sea-Tac airport book store and found his name on a tombstone printed on my book cover. Accompanied by his wife, Dr. John Tornow, no relation to the NW outlaw, attended the highly popular Oldtimer's Fair at Matlock in 1998. Note the misspelled word: "Fugitve."

book is well done, but it's terribly bloody. You have six murders, seven with the final shooting of John. What about introducing a little compassion, a bit of tenderness into the manuscript for contrast? I think that would be appreciated, especially by the gentle folks among your readers."

Leaving her office in dejection I began to reflect on what she had said. Another rewrite? I'd already spun my wheels for a month or so, removing the German vernacular. But there was some validity to her criticism, it was a brutal story. Any addition of tenderness or compassion would almost certainly have to be manufactured, fictionalized. But, what the heck, my fabricated dialogue already kept *Tornow* out of the non-fiction category. And how about the purists—the dyed-in-the-wool Tornow fans who, above all, insist on facts—not exaggeration and fantasy—as had been done so often in the past, to their disgust.

I agonized over the monumental decision for more than a week before I decided on another rewrite. But I wouldn't snippy-hootch the reader. I wanted to be right up front, explain what I'd done, and why. The book's Prologue carries the explanation, and my apology to "purist history buffs and disciples of bona fide Tornow memorabilia."

The recommended "tenderness and compassion" is derived from a platonic relationship between (actual) Minnie Tornow Bauer, and (my fictional) timber baron, John Kennedy. Minnie's husband, Henry Bauer (actual), seemed to have disappeared following the murder of their twin boys while they were bear hunting in September, 1911 (actual.) This gave me a logical point for inserting the fictional Kennedy, who showers Minnie with attention and romantic gifts throughout several chapters (fictional), something she had never experienced from her gruff old German husband. Enter tenderness and compassion as provided by fictional Kennedy.

The nineteen-month long pursuit of Tornow happened only

because the posse discovered a lean-to shack he had frequented, located near the boys' murder site. Although John was not at the lean-to, and was known to have revered the boys and his sister, the Sheriff issued a warrant to bring Tornow in for questioning. This scenario led to my selection of the book's title, *Guilty By Circumstance.*

Despite my explanation that the book is as factual as my research provided, *except* for fictional John Kennedy, and scenes where he is depicted, some readers may have missed that point in the Prologue. I recall one discussion of the book at a library club meeting. I'm often asked, "If John Tornow didn't kill the Bauer twins, who do you think did kill them?"

"Well, there were a couple of people who might have had a motive to shoot the twins. I just present the facts and then let the reader decide." Most people select one, or the other, from the two logical suspects. But one reader surprised us with his comment, "I think John Kennedy killed the boys," he said seriously.

This amateur sleuth didn't tumble to the error in his judgement, even following the titillating little chuckle that rippled through the audience following his "solution." I didn't burst his bubble by pointing out that fictional John Kennedy didn't even exist.

With the possibility of self-publishing *Tornow* becoming a closer reality, I donned my "worry" cap over one more segment of the book—culpability. How liable might I be over anything I've written? What would be the chances of a lawsuit—from any later generation Tornow—or from anybody?

Even in my pursuit of factual information, several situations seemed to carry strong implications, and a certain amount of judgement decisions by reporters and chroniclers of the past era. Whenever I detected this scenario jumping out at me from past written passages, I tried to soften the charges, or eliminate them entirely. The scribe who wrote the original piece is long gone, but I'm still around, still available to anyone who feels my words have aggrieved them.

Upon completing the *Tornow* manuscript, I made an extra copy and hauled it off to a prestigious law firm experienced in providing "manuscript insurance." Within a couple of weeks the lawmen issued their findings, and verbally reported, "We do not feel the book contains anything that would allow someone to successfully sue for libel. That is not to preclude a suit because it seems that in today's climate, everybody sues everybody else. But there is small risk of anybody mounting a successful suit."

Perhaps removal of the "non-fiction" label from the *Tornow* book might also have helped my cause. From another book where the author was being sued, came the finding: "It's exceedingly difficult to bring a successful libel claim arising out of a work of fiction." This from a story written by David Streitfeld in the "Washington Post."

I felt I was on safe legal ground with the *Tornow* book. Even a blind squirrel will occasionally find a nut.

Chapter 9

My wife Kit played a devil's advocate sounding board for me as we discussed the feasibility of self-publishing *Tornow*. Only problem, she acted more like a angelic advocate, exercising the positive. That's the role she plays in everyday life, too, always exemplifying her pragmatical inner self.

"What happens if we print all these books and aren't able to sell them?" I said, in a worried tone.

"Hasn't your input so far been positive?" she countered.

"Yes, but maybe people who aren't interested are reluctant to voice their negative opinions."

With a crafty kind of smile, she came back, "Well, I guess you'll just have to sell your book to *interested* readers."

Her homespun simplicity was mind-boggling. Someone had to worry about the consequences, about the worst-case scenario if we published and nobody came. So I told Kit I would bravely volunteer to worry for both of us.

"Bravo," she enthused, clapping her hands together in approval. "How did I know you would accept that challenge?"

"I suppose I could call Kurt Gorham just to find out what it would cost to print *Tornow*," I said.

He answered on the first ring. "Hi, Ron. What's goin' on? I know. You're out of the *Pete* book and you want us to print another thousand." That was Kurt, always displaying his unwavering optimism.

"You're half-right," I replied. "Yes, I'm almost out of *Pete* books, but I can't afford to sell anymore at five dollars while paying you seven. When's a good time to come talk with you about my Northwest outlaw book?"

"Would tomorrow be o.k.? No publisher response on the *Tornow* book, huh?"

"Oh, I've had lots of responses. So far, I've received a dozen, 'Not for us,' rejections; four, 'We choose not to pursue it with you;' A half-dozen just plain, 'Sorry;' even had one that said, 'We're not the right publisher for your book.' Yes, the mail has overflowed with responses—but no takers."

"Sure, come on up and let's see what we can put together on *Tornow*," Kurt concluded.

Having learned my disappointing monetary lesson on the *Pete* book, I was determined to do the *Tornow* book on a profitable basis—or not at all. *Pete* taught me the hard way that the experience curve could become a distressful non-profit bend in the literary highway. My financial objective resulted in the same well-worn dilemma. Two options—print a large quantity to bring down the price-per-book to a profitable level, or print fewer books, a quantity that I felt we could comfortably sell, but at a much higher price-per-book.

Kurt and I began negotiations by nailing down a few basics.

"How many pages are we talking about?" Kurt asked, finger poised in the air above his calculator.

"Less than *Pete*," I replied. "Probably about 45,000 words, with somewhere around twenty black and white photos."

"That should fit into 160-pages," Kurt quickly calculated.

"Yes, but it presents a problem," I muttered. "I want the book to retail at thirteen, or fourteen dollars, and from my research, most books in that price range are over 200-pages.

The difficulty is exactly the opposite of the *Pete* book. We purposely cut *Pete* down to 256-pages, yet we retailed it at $9.95, wholesaled at five bucks."

Lesson #214. Unlike spuds in the supermarket, books aren't sold ten pages for 99-cents.

In his calculating, Kurt smiled, a polite smile, yet it had the twinges of sarcasm, also. "It would be unfair of me to remind you that I thought the price of the *Pete* book was way too low. So I won't."

I lightly cuffed him alongside the head, "Yes, yes, I know, but I didn't care. *Pete* was a non-profit experiment, an obligation I had to fulfill. That was then. This is now."

"O.K.," Kurt said, "let's calculate 192-pages with twenty photos, and see what we come up with."

"Are you planning sixteen pages per run?" I asked. "If so, make it 208-pages and see what you get."

Banging his calculator with fingers that looked more accustomed to a shovel handle, Kurt soon looked up. "Got it," he smiled. "Two thousand books would come to $6736, or approximately $3.36 each. Can you live with that?"

"Two thousand?" I questioned, "that's quite a bunch, how much for just one thousand?"

"Now this is only a ballpark figure so don't hold me to it until it's fine-tuned. I come up with $4700, or approximately $4.70 per book. Quite a difference."

"Yes, too much difference," I squirmed, biting off each word for emphasis. "But how in hell would I ever sell two thousand books?" It was a monumental question with only ambiguous solutions.

Pushing his glasses back on his nose with a gesture of confident salesmanship, Kurt said, "Personally, Ron, I think you've got a very interesting and marketable book. You shouldn't have any trouble with two thousand, given sufficient time."

"Like the rest of my life?" I grinned.

It was obvious I would never crack the nut if the print cost was $4.70. Too many incidental expenses to pile on top of Kurt's charge.

I'd be right back in the unprofitable mode.

What to do? I experienced the pain of being impaled on the proverbial horns of a dilemma. The bottom-line was—two thousand, or nothing. I knew it would be a dice-roll; but I felt quite confident about the book, even though not a single agent or publisher had concurred.

"Well, Kurt, God hates a cowardly author. If you can draw up a contract at $6736 for two thousand, let's go for it. "Personally, I much prefer round numbers, why don't we make it an even $6700?

With some amount of feigned ceremony, I signed the contract and gave Kurt a check for the customary half-down.

"We need to start right away on that cover," Kurt said. "Let me get Kathy, my artist and layout specialist, and see if she has any good ideas."

I gave Kathy the photo of John Tornow's headstone while pointing out the misspelled, "fugitive."

"That's easy," the no-nonsense young lady said, "I'll correct the spelling. Let me play around with this cover layout and I'll get back to you in a couple of days. I think the epitaph needs an appropriate border."

We settled a few other minor questions about the book's cover and I wheeled Cherokee out the gravel lane toward home.

I usually do a lot of soul-searching after making a final decision on a monumental question. Once in awhile I'm reminded that I should step through those mental gymnastics *before* making the big decision. All the brainwork had left me drained. Even the ends of my hair were tired.

In just a short while I came to the creek used as a reference point in Kurt's directions. This time, no cow, not the brown one, or the black and white one either. Oh, oh, an omen? I shrugged it off while making the right-hand turn. Out ahead was just an empty field except for a few blackbirds trying to make a living.

On that warm summer afternoon my concentration certainly was not on driving, not on the lush green, bottomland foliage, nor the old-fashioned farm homes that lined the drive, not even on the roiled, whirling current of the picturesque Chehalis River that raced Cherokee alongside the road. Instead, my mind was identifying and sequencing the multitude of tasks that required attention during the ensuing 4-6 weeks before *Tornow* rolled off the press.

I knew the initial priority projects would be developing publicity. People would want to know about the book and its availability. We needed lots of hype before we hit the streets. I wanted a launching pad; a location where the book would first be made available, and where I could inaugurate my first signings. Swanson's three supermarkets had done a commendable launch on the *Pete* book; they deserved the debut for *Tornow*, also. And I liked those 3 col.x10-inch publicity ads they ran with my picture, signing dates, and a splash of colorful verbiage about the outlaw.

Most residents of the nearby counties knew the John Tornow story which surfaces about every ten years as newspapers run feature articles on the accused killer. Native resident, Chuck Swanson certainly knew the story and needed no salesmanship from me.

"Sure, Ronnie, we'll sponsor and advertise the signings, when do you want to do it?" Chuck asked.

"Books will be available August 11th, let's do it on Friday, August 22nd, Aberdeen store in the morning, Hoquiam in the afternoon. I'll have time to do South Aberdeen the first week in September."

"Sounds good, what's the retail price?" Chuck asked.

"It will sell at $13.95, and you will receive your usual liberal wholesale price," I told my grocer friend of almost fifty-years. Chuck had been my mentor in 1948 when I first jumped into the wholesale grocery business.

Lesson #215. Good business friends can enhance the success of self-publishing authors. Especially if they buy a book!

Just a few words about newspaper advertising at this point. Retailers who do a lot of advertising pay considerably less per column-inch of space than a casual customer like down-and-out authors such as me. Just a fact of life. Them what got it pay less—them what don't got it, like me, pay more.

Swanson's ran an excellent ad with book title, my picture, signing dates and times. The 3x10 ad would have cost me in the neighborhood of $500.00 in the local daily paper. But a large advertiser at the newspaper's best rate would only pay around $200.00 for the same ad. High volume has its own reward.

Even so, it was a good investment. Store profits on the books sold during the signings exceeded the advertising expense many times over.

The next step was to contact the local daily paper's news editor, whom I had known for several years. When I told him my *Tornow* book would soon be on the street, he was willing to run a feature article on the outlaw. The story headline read: "Former local man recounts tragic story of fugitive Tornow," with a reproduction of the book's cover, signing dates and times. Those types of news feature articles are invaluable to selling books and booksignings, especially for unknown authors like some of us are.

Each time I contacted a local newspaper (twelve feature stories, only one turndown, excluding Seattle) I gave them a brief, two-page "press release," plus an assortment of 6-8 black & white photos that I had used in the book. I believe that approach was successful because it focused on the incredible story of John Tornow, highly interesting to the paper's readers, with, "Oh, by the way, a book about the outlaw has just been published and you can pick one up at the following locations..."

Another favorable aspect of my providing the story and photos, which were usually returned to me after publication; it was a timesaver for the editor. My press releases were written somewhat professionally so, in many instances, the editors could print them as written. The pictures also "dressed up" the articles. They were mostly 3x5-inches, some 4x6, and a few 5x7's. Cost was negligible when I had them printed on a "Special" drugstore promotion. Recycling them also helped salvage the budget.

With the book's initial blast-off scheduled at the supermarket, I drew an approximate 20-mile circle around the launch-point and began contacting other potential outlets and advertisers. Back in my hometown, the biggest supermarket, Pick-Rite Thriftway, and the weekly newspaper supported the book like Swanson's and the daily paper had.

Next, I felt it was important to reach an agreement with Dick Moulton, the Montesano book distributor who had placed the *Pete* book with several of his retail customers. Dick and I concurred that I would only place opening inventories with a limited few customers where signings had been scheduled. Following the initial placements, Dick would then control inventories of *Pete* or *Tornow* with any retail customers he normally serviced. As in the past, I would continue to handle all publicity.

At this time, I recognized the importance of "signing up" the two major Seattle book distributors. With the demise of Pacific Pipeline, a large book wholesaler, Partners, the Michigan-based firm had opened a warehouse, as previously announced, in Renton, Washington, a suburb of Seattle. The new distributor was identified as Partners/West. These folks were the key to getting *Tornow* into major bookstores such as Border's, Barnes & Noble, Waldenbooks and Crown.

With only a printed *Tornow* bookcover from Gorham as my sales tool, I made an appointment with the Partners/West head buyer. Unaccustomed to Renton or Seattle traffic and locations, the new book distributor's office/warehouse was as hard to find as an atheist in church.

Arriving at the appointed time, I found the buyer to be a young, affable executive who attentively listened to my sales pitch.

"This is my second self-published book, the first one having sold out its initial printing. *Guilty By Circumstance* is a true story about a Northwest outlaw, John Tornow, the accused killer of six men around the turn of the century. He eluded capture for nineteen months in the thick forests of the Olympic Mountains. Books will be off the press on August 11th. I plan to market the major local booksellers, and Partners would be the logical supplier."

In my presentations I claimed the book to be a "true" story about Tornow's life even though it was classified as fiction. Again, everything was factual except for the dialogue, and the fictional John Kennedy. I still found it difficult to resign myself to accept the "fiction" designation.

"It sounds good to me, Ron. I'll have you complete one of our standard wholesale agreement forms, then mail it back to me. Also, let me know of any signings you schedule so we can deliver books on time. When you receive the *Tornow* book from the printer, call me with the case count (number of books packed to a standard case), and I'll give you a purchase order in even case multiples."

"What are your terms of payment?" I asked, knowing it would be an established price without negotiation.

"We pay 55% off retail, payment to you ninety-days following sales we make to retailers," he replied.

I knew the terms would be hard and fast—or maybe better phrased, "hard and slow." Ninety day terms were a country mile slower than my accustomed, "two-percent cash, net 14 days" in the grocery trade. Also, the 55% was brutal, but as I learned later, somewhat standard in the book business. At 55%, my $13.95 retail book would pay me $6.28 at wholesale. Ouch! Also, this major book wholesaler paid authors/publishers ninety-days *after* a sale to a retailer. I delivered books to Partners in August, my first check wouldn't arrive until mid-December. Snortin' old haywire! It would be soggy beans and tattered trousers for awhile, but it was my only avenue for selling to the major bookstores.

Some supermarkets and various other booksellers were being serviced by Seattle-based now defunct Adams News Co., Inc. I called their book buyer (as opposed to periodicals), Mr. Steve Linville, and made an appointment.

Here again, I was cordially received and sold Adams on handling my book. Steve called in one of their marketing experts and we discussed possible book events. By this time I knew the case count was 52 books.

"Why don't we plan a promotion at the Sea-Tac Airport book store as soon as the books are available," Steve told the sales expert. "We'll make a mass display in the window."

Wow! This would be a terrific meltdown inauguration for *Tornow*. The Sea-Tac Airport book store was a mass-people location.

Steve thwacked away at his computer, giving me a purchase order for 312 books, or six cases. It was the largest single order for books I received—before, during, after, or at any time whatsoever. At least half of the books went into the airport display. A couple of weeks after I'd delivered the six cases to Adams, Steve called me asking that I go to the bookstore and sign the books in the display. "They sell better if signed," he assured me.

When I arrived at the store, they had featured the book in a mass display on a table, with just a few remaining in the window. As I signed, my fingers cramped to let me know that three cases of books were quite a few to autograph. Still quite naive in the business, I later realized I should have spent a full day at the bookstore with personal on-the-spot signing. I also found out that having the author in-house usually perked up sales of that particular book.

Adams News paid for the books on a different program than Partners/West. They paid about the same wholesale price but ninety-days after I delivered books to their *warehouse*, as opposed to ninety-days after Partners sold to their *retailers*.

This was greatly appreciated and helped speed up my cash flow.

I began beating the drum for as much publicity as I could get, even before the books became available. I had contacted several radio stations, suggesting their talk-show hosts might consider interviews with me detailing the life of John Tornow and publicizing the upcoming signings. My first interview was on Aberdeen's KBKW on July 30th, KH2O Tacoma on September 5th, and later on Aberdeen's KXRO. The interviews went well and I think were quite interesting for the stations' audiences.

Thank goodness for my Toastmaster's training. As explained, it doesn't eliminate the butterflies from public speaking, it only trains them to fly in formation.

By this time, we were moving along like Atlas Van Lines, and I had yet to see the first copy of *Tornow*.

Lesson #216. Even if you have to mortgage the baby, getting your name and the book title publicized is vitally important.

When I had time on my hands, I obtained lists of all major bookstore locations in Western Washington State. I mailed each of them an inexpensive promotional flyer advising the *Tornow* book would be available through one of the distributors around the end of August. I mentally calculated——the sale of only four books through this mass mailing would pay the postage and stationery expense. It also opened the door to a few more signing sessions.

With this mailing, I had stepped out of my imaginary twenty-mile circle drawn from the kickoff signings in Aberdeen and Hoquiam. I was quite certain the book would enjoy greater sales in the towns and neighborhoods in close proximity to Tornow's home stompin' ground—the Matlock community. It made sense that book sales should be proportionately better in towns like Aberdeen, Hoquiam, Montesano, Olympia and Shelton, or so I projected. In general, my predictions were correct. I didn't think that sales in larger cities—Tacoma and Seattle—would go as well. Difficulty in obtaining publicity, most people were unfamiliar with the *Tornow* story, and the increased competition were all factors that constricted urban sales. However we enjoyed limited success in a few tucked away pockets in the city suburbs. The bigger cities could not be, indeed never had been, totally ignored when we distributed *Tornow*.

Around the end of July, Kurt called. "We've got galley proofs of *Guilty By Circumstance* for your approval or corrections. I'll put 'em in the mail today. If no major problems, we'll go to press after you return them to us. Run up the flag!" Kurt yelled, "John Tornow is about to be immortalized in first book form."

The text was almost flawless. Kit and I chuckled over one minor typo. A line, "..sprawling 160-acre homestead," came out, "...sprawling l-acre homestead."

"One-acre doesn't sprawl very much," Kit grinned. "Maybe the Tornows raised miniature fruit trees and low-bush beans."

We had discussed photo placement in the book several times and found it impossible to position pictures on the same page as the corresponding text. Hoping finally to at least get "close by," we divided the book pages into thirds, then earmarked each photo either first-third, second-third, or last-third. Gorham then placed them sequentially.

We were receiving top-notch publicity on the outside for supermarket signings; separate freestanding ads; placement within the retailer's grocery ad; feature articles in local newspapers; and radio talk-show interviews. But I felt there was one promo opportunity we were overlooking, "in-store" promotion a week or so prior to the actual signings. I'd learned that from watching how Barnes & Noble operated.

I traipsed back to Kinko's to have them typeset a sign we could display the week prior to a signing. I purposely had the sign wording done generically so the signs could be recycled in various stores.

Here's what I did. The signs measured 11x17-inches, the master copy was on white paper, which I then ran on bright-colored card stock on Kinko's in-house copy machines. First line printed across the top was—"Come and Meet..;" then bigger letters, second line, "Author Ron Fowler..;" third line, smaller letters, "In Our Store;" with fourth and fifth lines left open for specific, individualized information.

Next I left a large blank space. For each signing I hand-lettered a smaller sign giving day, date and time of signing. This small sign was taped or stapled into the blank space, and later replaced for the next signing.

On the bottom, right-hand quarter of the sign I taped a 4x6-inch colored photo of my mug. Kit had taken the original photo. Reprints (on special) cost around fifty-cents. My photo was also recycled except for the one where someone added a mustache and flowing beard with a black pen. Not a good likeness. I threw it away.

The wording in the left-hand bottom quarter said: "Ron will sign and discuss his latest book, *Guilty By Circumstance,* the amazing story of Northwest outlaw John Tornow."

These signs provided advance notice of upcoming book signings in supermarkets. They were displayed in-store three weeks ahead so customers could schedule their attendance, should they so desire.

COME AND MEET...
AUTHOR, RON FOWLER
IN OUR STORE

SATURDAY
SEP. 5TH
NOON To 4:00 PM

RON WILL SIGN
AND DISCUSS HIS
LATEST BOOK,

"GUILTY BY
CIRCUMSTANCE"

THE AMAZING STORY
OF FAMOUS NORTHWEST
WILDERNESS OUTLAW
JOHN TORNOW.

After the master copy was made I could make cardstock copies for around thirty-cents each. Many were used 3-4 times, just adding updated dates and times for subsequent signings.

In the larger supermarkets I tried to display three of the signs in prominent locations around the store about 7-10 days prior to the signing. If it wasn't convenient for me to be at a distant store ahead of the signing, I mailed the signs and store personnel did a fair job of putting them up. On several occasions, however, I was reminded of the old adage; "If you want something done right, do it yourself."

These signing announcement signs alerted the shoppers in each store that a signing was going to be held. Cost of the dozen or so signs I had made—typesetting and my color photos, didn't exceed twenty-bucks.

Another worthwhile sign we made was just a simple cutout of the newspaper feature articles describing John Tornow, the book, etc. We taped the clippings onto similar 11x17 cardstock, usually with the newspaper's masthead and date across the top, put a cardboard strongback on the poster board so it would stand up. I used these as "attention-getters" on the tables or counters during signings. I think people usually remembered reading the newspaper article, recognized it on the table, then stopped by and bought a book. (Sometimes.)

Pre-planning pays big dividends. First we did the preliminary publicity, distribution, contracts and personal legwork in the allotted time span. We found that the sequence and timing meant everything.

This massive display of Guilty By Circumstance near front-end checkout location at Top Food and Drug supermarket in Edmonds sold more than fifty books.

Like Hannibal trudging over the Alps with his elephants in 218 B.C., we had big things pushing us over the top also.

Just wait 'til we get the books!

Chapter 10

In mid-August, we entertained company from Mexico and I needed to pick up books at Gorhams. We combined sightseeing at Mt. St. Helens with a side trip to my favorite printer.

Like a desolate moonscape, the near hills and far mountainsides were almost devoid of vegetation, birds, or animals; blanketed with volcanic ash, barren and gray.

"The trees that fell down all died in the same direction?" Guillermo queried from the backseat of Kit's car.

"Yes, the volcanic blast erupted to the north, knocking the tall timber down like matchsticks," I explained. We had met our house guests in Monterrey, Mexico while on one of our I.E.S.C. projects.

Mid-August, the sun radiated a sizzling blanket. Only noontime and already it was above ninety degrees. Driving along the narrow mountain highway, shimmering heat rays danced above the asphalt. My face was hot and dry, my nose rebelled at the lingering acrid smell of the volcanic dust.

"How's the temperature?" I inquired of Guillermo and his wife Aurora, hoping I could bump up the air conditioning a notch.

Enjoying our unusual Northwest heat wave that produced Mexico-like weather, our guests still wore sweaters while Kit and I were in short-sleeved cotton shirts.

"We're fine," Guillermo smiled. "These temperatures is just purr-fect for us."

Inconspicuously, I tapped the AC button up one more click,

hoping our warm-blooded guests wouldn't notice the slight cooling effect. The outside reading registered 92-degrees on the car's computer screen, 80 degrees inside. It was getting hotter; and so were we Washingtonians.

Driving back to the freeway I announced, "We may have to stop and pick up books from my printer on the way home. He thought they would be ready today."

"Where will you put them?" Kit asked. There's not much room in the trunk with our luggage."

"I won't pick up all 2,000 books, but I'll take whatever we can squeeze in."

"Sure, Ron," Guillermo said, raising his voice above the freeway rumble, "we have much room back here for many books. Me and Aurora can...how do you say it...smooch..together very tight."

I called Kurt from a roadside phone. "Come on out, they're ready to go. Dick Moulton stopped and picked up three boxes. He said it was your idea," Kurt told me.

"I've got passengers so I can't take all of them, but I'll plan to pick up the balance in a day or so."

The winding blacktop road to Gorham's through the fertile river valley gave our guests a glimpse of Northwest farm country.

"It's so green and lush," Guillermo said.

"Verde y muy bonito," Aurora commented in Spanish. Her command of English was not as proficient as her husband's. When conversing she usually spoke Spanish to Guillermo who in turn would translate, "Aurora says..."

Making our right-hand turn, I noticed both cows stood beside the creek. Thinking it would be a rather complicated story, I decided not to pass along the tale of the brown one, or the black and white one either for that matter.

Kurt sat on a stool in the shade of his print shop building. "Whew, it's too hot to work in there," he said, standing up at our arrival.

I introduced our guests then began to rearrange trunk luggage.

Kurt wheeled out ten boxes of books, then waited to determine our capacity.

Immediately, I opened one of the boxes and held up a copy of *Guilty By Circumstance*. I'll remember that moment forever, my first glimpse of my pride and joy. It was beautiful, but would we be able to sell all 2,000 copies? It really didn't matter at that point. I'd already decided that was the project we'd do or die on.

We began loading, a few boxes in the trunk, some in the backseat which would crowd our Mexican friends. In the stifling heat we worked at a pace tempting cardiac arrest.

"I hope you and Aurora have enough space to sit back comfortably," I told Guillermo.

"No problema," he grinned. "Now I get much close to my wife," as he pinched her arm, drawing a broad smile.

We managed to load the ten boxes Kurt had wheeled out, but no more.

"I'll pick up the balance on Wednesday or Thursday," I told Kurt, perspiring from every orifice. "Must be getting old," I gasped, "I'm almost out of puff."

As I climbed behind the wheel and drove out the country lane, I could feel rivulets of perspiration trickling down my neck and onto my shirt. I was clammy and sticky from the exertion in ninety-degree temperatures. How good it would feel to turn up the air conditioning.

Seeming to read my mind, Guillermo asked, "Ron, would you mind putting up the window? It is become quite breezy back here for us."

Early the next day Kit and I loaded our guests and their luggage for the trip to Seattle's Sea-Tac airport where they had been scheduled out at 8:00 a.m. We said our goodbyes at the gate, then headed for my first wholesale distributor where I made out a duplicate receipt form for six boxes—312 books. At the next wholesaler, as per an earlier agreement, I consigned three boxes, 156 books.

Several weeks prior, I had solicited an order from one of Seattle's largest independent book stores. The burbly young Community Events Coordinator had agreed to take twenty-five books on consignment and display them in-store, but only if I would schedule a reading/signing session with her.

Having already contacted several Seattle area radio stations and newspapers and getting considerably less than tremendous response, I felt reluctant to hold a signing at the large store with just limited publicity. But, what could I say? This place sold books, a lot of books, and I had books to sell. I signed on the dotted line, agreeing to a personal appearance on August 27th, two weeks hence.

"You'll bring more books with you when you come?" the young coordinator asked. "We'll probably need more than this twenty-five for your signing."

Back home, later that day, I called Al Calisewski. "Have you had your nap?" I inquired.

"Just finished, now I'm watching the Mariners get beat," Al said.

"Hey, what are you doing tomorrow? Gorham finished printing the books and there's still about 1300 at his place for me to pick up. Do you want to go with me tomorrow to get them, then distribute a few to customers?"

"That beats sitting around watching the water evaporate from my fish tank," he replied.

"You don't have a fish tank."

"That must be why it evaporated so fast," he said.

I picked Al up at his townhouse before 7:00 a.m., and it was easy to see he was eager for the trip. He met me outside his back door, impatiently bouncing from one oxford-clad foot, to the other.

"I'm early, and you're waiting outside, how come?"

"Because I'm kinda getting into this book-selling thing," he replied. "How do they look? Do you have one?"

"On the backseat," I jerked my thumb behind us.

"Hey, that's all right," he beamed. "I might even buy one," Al grinned.

Out we went, down I-5, over to Rochester, past the two-cow creek, back onto the country lane to Gorham's.

The first printing was for 2,000, plus an overrun of twenty-four books. Dick Moulton had wanted to get a quick start distributing so I let him pick up 156 from Kurt. In the first load I had picked up 520, leaving a total remaining of 1,348.

Cherokee seemed to scowl a bit at the weight, but we managed to squeeze in all twenty-six boxes.

"That's a load." Kurt quipped. "Any more and Al would have had to hitchhike home."

We delivered a total of 250 books to the three Swanson's supermarkets. They would have about a week to sell from their displays before the signings on August 22nd. We put up our in-store signs publicizing the signings. The newspaper article had already appeared and a certain feeling led me to believe we'd sell a few books even before the signing.

Al and I distributed another case of books to retailers in and around Montesano before hitting the backroad to Shelton, Tornow-territory. Earlier, I had lined up a signing at the major regional chain supermarket, so I delivered fifty books to them. Billie Howard at the Shelton-Mason County Historical Museum took twenty, because of the historical significance within the local area. Jim and Laurie at the tiny Matlock General Store also wanted twenty, with a dozen dropped off at a Shelton restaurant/tavern. Another downtown supermarket also took twelve.

Shelton had been the nearest town to the Tornow escapades. Al commented, "The book should sell here like gangbusters."

Cherokee almost sighed with relief at the reduced tonnage.

That afternoon on the trip home, Al said, "Not bad, we got rid of more than four-hundred books during this first day."

"Yes, at least we put them into the stores, but that doesn't necessarily mean they're sold," I cautioned him. "Remember, the books are all on consignment. We can't count our Tornows until money crosses our palms."

One day the following week, prior to doing my daily thirty-minutes on the treadmill (squirrel cage), I peered outside at the dull, overcast August morning. Just my luck, I thought inwardly, my first *Tornow* book signing and it looked like rain, unseasonal for August, even in the rain capital of the Northwest.

Thickening gray murkiness depressed that Friday morning as I wheeled into Al's parking area. We'd left early so we'd have time for coffee with Chuck Swanson before the signing began.

Ninety minutes, and 75-miles later, Chuck spotted us at the market's front door, our arms loaded with signs, extra books and the paraphernalia from which books are sold.

"Here comes Ronnie and Calahoosky," Chuck proclaimed, beaming his usual smile, a Swedish twinkle in his eyes. I cringed at the pet names.

"Can we buy you a cup of coffee at the snack bar?" Al asked.

"Sure, men, let me have a quick word with Phyllis in the office. You go on over, pour the coffee and save me a seat."

With that, he skipped upstairs like a youngster not half his eighty-plus years.

I noticed my signing table was set up and dozens of *Tornow* books were displayed. A fellow dressed in jeans and T-shirt with his back toward us stood inspecting a book. We stepped in his direction and Al said, loud enough for the customer to hear, "Looks like we've got our first prospect."

The man wheeled around towards Al, smiled, and asked, "Oh, are you the author?"

"I'm not but you might try this guy," Al said, pointing my way.

"Hi, I'm Ron Fowler. That book is about John Tornow, the Northwest outlaw."

"Yes, I'm familiar with the story. My grandfather knew him well."

Well maybe, I thought. It seemed that almost everyone's grandfather had been on a first-name basis with John, and that was 85-years ago.

"I'd like to buy a book if you'll autograph it for me," he said.

"Be glad to," I replied, "maybe I can personalize it to you."

"That would be great, my name's Dugan."

Ten minutes before advertised start time, a half-dozen customers stood around the signing table; some were flipping pages, others had made their decision and stood waiting to have me sign their books. It was interesting to watch people's reactions. A few knew what they wanted, picked up a book, thrust it at me for my signature. The crowd around the table seemed to attract other customers out of curiosity. The indecisive people might ask a dozen questions, then wait ten or fifteen minutes before buying or walking away. Others who knew what they came for, wasted no time as they dug into wallets or purses.

At all of my signings at retail locations, I thought it best to have customers pay for the books at the regular checkstands instead of buying directly from me. Personal checks and credit cards were best handled by the professional cashiers.

This also eliminated any possible monetary misunderstandings with the retailers who were earning a profit on the book. The only downside was the possibility of a customer sidestepping the checkstands and forgetting to pay for the book. In nearly all stores we located strategically near the cashiers, and also the exits, so it was easy to make sure book-buyers actually bought books.

Lesson #217. Don't handle someone else's bucks in a retail store.

My signing arm knew we'd pumped a goodly number of customers through the checkstands at the end of the two-hour session. Former friends and neighbors stopped by. Most bought a book, others bought two or three for gifts. Some people I hadn't seen in years but I couldn't take time to talk with them because of other customers standing patiently in line. I hoped they understood. "Hey, this was great," Al said. "You sold 58 books in two hours."

We grabbed a quick sandwich at the supermarket's snack bar, then jumped into Cherokee for the three-mile drive to Swanson's Hoquiam store where we were scheduled at 1:00 p.m.

Store Manager, Doug King greeted us on arrival. "Ron, a lady bought three of your books, left them in this sack for you to sign, said she couldn't be here this afternoon."

"We can do that all day," I smiled at him. Several store employees, who were acquaintances, were among book buyers that afternoon. Once again, I was kept busy signing for most of the scheduled three-hour event.

Al stood talking with prospective customers while I brandished my trusty pen. He knew the Tornow story well, so he did a magnificent job of explaining the local interest and convincing customers to buy once they meandered to our table.

The weather had remained overcast most of the day, but on the drive home a few rays of August sunshine broke through the cloudy sky. I could smell the warmth of daytime dampness meeting the late afternoon sun. "You should feel quite satisfied about your first *Tornow* signings," Al offered as Cherokee moved us down the freeway through the dissipating grayness.

"I'm more than satisfied. If the book goes this well every place, we shouldn't have any problem selling out the first printing."

During the initial two weeks of displaying the book, Swanson's stores sold a total of 226 copies, including two signings, even before the September session at the South Aberdeen store. I was overwhelmed, never having imagined it would do that well.

The next day Montesano distributor, Dick Moulton had scheduled me back at Pick-Rite Thriftway in Montesano, my "growing up" town. I appreciated the tremendous turnout of friends, shirttail relatives and former acquaintances, some I hadn't seen since schooldays, fifty-years ago.

Once again, the supermarket's management had run a free-standing ad in the local weekly paper announcing the book and the signing session. I barely had time for a cup of coffee during the two-hour stint.

At this event I had the pleasure of my first meeting with a descendant of the Northwest outlaw, a totally unexpected delight, a fateful encounter. Mid-morning a young lady approached our signing table.

"I'd like to buy two books," she said, "one for me, one for my brother."

"Sure," I smiled, "I can personalize them for you. What's your name?"

"Sarah."

"O.K., is it spelled, S-a-r-a-h?"

"Yes, that's correct."

"And what's your last name, Sarah?"

"Tornow," she said nonchalantly.

I stared wide-eyed in astonishment. Regaining my composure, I asked, "How are you related to John Tornow?"

"His brother, Edward, was my great grandfather," she said.

"But we don't talk about it much because people seem to look down on us when we tell them we're Tornows."

"I think you should be very proud of it," I replied. "Your ancestors were leading figures in a most important aspect of Northwest history. Don't pay any attention to those short-sighted individuals."

Here again, I wanted to spend more time talking to her; asking about her family, where she was from. But the line was six deep and before I could ask her to stay awhile, she'd melded into the supermarket crowd. It all happened so quickly, I'm not even sure if her name was Sarah, but I had the last name correct.

Two hours, thirty-six books sold. Al and I moved on to the next supermarket signing Dick Moulton had arranged in the nearby town of Elma. The newspaper was a supplemental weekly printed by the *Daily* in Aberdeen. The advance publicity was less than we'd enjoyed at our previous signings, primarily no early P.R. by the supermarket.

As mentioned earlier, Ted Rakoski had provided me with a key picture of the entire Tornow family. He lived nearby and attended the Elma session to needle me once again for misspelling his name in the first printing.

"There definitely is no "W" in my family's name," he reminded me.

Reduced publicity resulted in reduced sales. As I recall we sold seventeen books at the Elma event.

On August 26th, a Tuesday, we ventured farther afield.

Dick Moulton had again scheduled a supermarket signing; this time in a small town about fifty-miles in the opposite direction, away from Matlock. It was a weekday, a population not familiar with the story, and with almost no advance publicity. We bombed!

I think we sold three books; one to the store owner, another to a friend who lived in the town. I can't remember who bought the third one.

We got "outta Dodge" with our tails between our legs.

That afternoon, we drove back to Aberdeen at a Moulton-inspired gift/mail order shop where we sold about a dozen with limited publicity. Altogether it was a bombed-out day.

Speaking of "bombed," my next signing was an event we chuckle about today, although it was not humorous at the time.

You'll remember the high-volume, Seattle-area bookstore where the Events Coordinator insisted I do a reading/signing as a condition for stocking and displaying the book. I knew my act needed testing in a metropolitan setting, but I had misgivings over the lack of publicity. A "liner" had appeared in the book events column of a local newspaper, nothing more.

It was an hour's drive from home, scheduled for Wednesday at 7:00 p.m. Kit agreed to go along for company. We arrived about thirty-minutes prior to the event, nothing new about that. The co-ordinator, let's call her Elaine so that revealing her identity won't embarrass her, or me, anymore than I already was. She was a Mary Poppins look-alike, sprightly and cheerful, attributes so typical of the young, and the young at heart.

"Hi, Elaine, are we all set for the signing?" I asked when I spotted her at a checkstand.

"I'm looking forward to it," she warbled.

This place was probably the biggest bookstore I'd ever visited. Two floors, plus a basement, zillions of books, but sparse of customers.

"Where did you display my book?" I asked out of curiosity.

"It's over here, follow me."

We arrived at the "Northwest" section. There it was! What a thrill to find your very own book displayed in a first-class metropolitan bookstore.

I counted books. Dismayed, I told Elaine, "Not very good, you've only sold one."

"Oh, I've got it," she said sheepishly. "I wanted to read it before your session tonight so I could ask intelligent questions." That made it even worse. "Come over to the front of the store. I'll show you where we set up for our guest authors."

What a perfect setting. This humongous store in a heavily-populated area, an ornate oak lectern displaying a placard announcing the book with signing/reading date and time, and about thirty comfortable chairs in an oval arrangement for the audience yet to arrive.

Glancing at her watch, Elaine said, "We're still about ten minutes early. People will soon start to drift in," she said in her cheery voice. I wondered about that.

It was late summer and as I recall, the evening had turned a bit blustery—as Seattle's weather occasionally does. Kit and I sat at the end of one of the three rows of chairs. I leaned over and whispered, "If nobody shows up, it will provide a good excuse to just get out of here. I've been afraid this might happen in the big city."

My watch had ticked over to five after seven. No attendance, but we could save our embarrassing souls by just scooting out of there. Elaine walked toward us. At the same time I spied a sparrowlike, little, old lady dressed in a heavy coat coming through the front door. Seeing the empty chairs, she walked over and plunked herself down in row three.

Drat the luck, I thought. This probably constitutes an audience. It was time to introduce myself so I ambled over to where my audience-of-one was seated.

"Good evening," I purred, trying to disguise my consternation at not being able to go A.W.O.L. "My name is Ron Fowler. I am the author of this book about a Northwest outlaw." I made it short and brief, trying not to pique her curiosity.

"Oh my, how interesting," she chirped. "I'm visiting here from Kansas, and I just came in to get out of the inclement weather. Didn't know you had an author event going on, but I'll stay. Goodness, I'm so lucky. Maybe I'll learn something about your outlaw. You say his name was Don Tornow? Besides, it's more comfortable in here than it is outside tonight."

I reluctantly shuffled to the podium, turned and faced my audience of three. There sat Kit who came because I asked her; Elaine, because she was "on the clock;" and Miss Heavy Coat who was there to avoid the weather. What a stimulating group!

I had prepared about thirty-minutes of introduction and a synopsis of my *Tornow* book. For that evening I shortened the program to fifteen-minutes, after which I asked if there were any questions from the "audience."

Elaine surprised me when she asked, "Were there any potential suspects in the murders of John and William Bauer, other than John Tornow?"

Wow! That question ambushed me. She *really* had read the book. I answered her question and she bounced right back with,

"What ever happened to Minnie Tornow Bauer after her husband, Henry, disappeared?"

The perky Events Coodinator fired questions at me for fifteen minutes. Compared with any of my later audience participants, the young lady impressed me as having done a thorough job of developing questions, more thought-provoking than any others, and I complimented her meticulous preparation.

Miss Heavy Coat just sat there, said not a word. Finally, she stood up, commenting, "My gracious, it's getting late and the weather appears to have improved." With that, she strolled out the front door just as casually as she had entered.

Later, Kit commented, "At least she could have bought a book."

And that's how we became "sales-less" in Seattle.

The author spoke to a large group of Hoquiam High School history students who were interested in the John Tornow story. Pictured here, Fowler is autographing books purchased by students.

Chapter 11

"I think John Tornow carried this dime in his pocket," Dana Anderson said, "but I want you to have it as a keepsake in recognition of the book you wrote about his life." He then handed me the 1904 Liberty head dime.

Dana was a Tornow afficionado from Matlock. With tons of determination and a metal-detector, he pinpointed the exact wilderness location of John's 1913 campsite at the lake. Among the broken pieces of turn-of-the-century metal debris, he had unearthed the dime. Of course, it could have been dropped by a deputy after the shoot-out, but I'd rather think it's authentic Tornow, my treasured piece of historic memorabilia.

President Rand Iversen and the dedicated board members of the Mary M. Knight historical program, organizers and caretakers of the museum, provided valuable documentation and support for my *Tornow* book. In turn, I dedicated it to their worthy cause, pledging a contribution to their program of twenty-five cents for each book sold. As this is being written, and the books have nearly sold out, my total donation has exceeded $1,200.00. In addition, the board members contracted for more than 70 books at wholesale, each member selling them for retail ($13.95) thereby adding another $500.00 to their treasury. The astute members also reckoned on the twenty-five cents additional received for each copy they sold.

Perhaps the most successful book signing event I experienced with *Tornow* was on August 29th at a major Shelton supermarket.

Al Calisewski, right, and author are pictured while hunting artifacts at the recently discovered Tornow campsite near the Wynooche River in Grays Harbor County. Calisewski is a long-time friend of the author and distributed many copies of the Tornow book to Western Washington retailers.

This huge store was the mother of all supermarkets, at least for a Shelton-size town. The signing had been publicized by a major John Tornow feature article in the local weekly newspaper, but no freestanding ads were run. On that Friday a continual stream of shoppers poured through the market. I estimated close to 5,000 customers passed by our signing table in the lobby during the three-hour session. In hindsight, I should have scheduled the event for all day. We only stopped a minuscule number of the total shoppers, but in doing so sold more than 70 books. *Tornow* was also sold from the market's book rack for more than six months. They were serviced by one of the Seattle distributors so I have no record of their total sales, but I would guess it topped 150 books, including a second signing session in December. No mean feat, that.

Relaxing in my recliner while steepling my fingers and mentally evaluating our sales at various locations, all of a sudden it hit me like a meteor from the galaxy. Our "meat and potatoes" retailers were supermarkets. And why? High volume shopper traffic—lots of people in and out. With, or without signings, on an everyday basis, *Tornow* was selling better, much better, in supermarkets who probably had ten times, maybe a hundred times more daily customers than the average bookstore. Perhaps if I'd been a much-publicized author just out with a new book, customers might have trooped to their favorite bookstore for a copy. But little-knowns like me have to earn our sales the old-fashioned way, selling books where the foot traffic is, along with the daily necessities found at such markets, like bread, milk, lettuce and video rentals.

For the first few months, *Tornow* sales were better than we could have ever hoped for. Al usually went with me and the miles began to pile up on Cherokee. We averaged two signing/reading sessions a week. When "selling" a prospective customer for a book-signing session, I don't recall one actual turndown. Again, on a consignment program, where the retailer didn't pay until the books were sold, it was a win/win for the store. My only obligation, after committing to self-publishing, was my time—plus mileage. Requests for my appearance were pouring in from bookstores, libraries, supermarkets, fraternal organizations and writer's clubs.

As we busied ourselves selling books and earning our keep, a funny thing happened via the U.S. mail. You may recall, I had literary lawyers review *Tornow* to determine my susceptibility from a libel suit. Their findings provided a renewed comfort level. Then, in mid-October, an envelope arrived that sent shock waves down through my stubby wooden pencil and reams of yellow paper. I read the return address before opening the envelope. I felt more like slitting my wrists with the letter opener, than slitting open the envelope. In the extreme, left-hand, upper corner, I read: From, Thomas T. Tornow, Attorney-at-Law, Whitefish, Montana. It had happened! What's the prison sentence for libel or slander?

I knew it had to be done. With quivering fingers, I opened the envelope. Strange. Just a short message: "I enjoyed reading your book. How might I locate a copy of the "Ballad of John Tornow?" Signed, Thomas T. Tornow. I breathed a huge sigh of relief.

A former Matlock-ite, Tom Roberson, had written a song about John Tornow, and sang it accompanied by his own guitar-strumming. I had a copy of the lyrics, so sending them was no problem. The big question was how Tom Tornow had laid his hands on a copy of the book when our distribution had been limited to Western Washington. Curiosity killed the cat and it may have stripped away a few calendar months from this old Tom, too, but I had to know.

Brimming with said curiosity and displaying willpower strong as a bowl of melted Jello, I could no longer resist the temptation. I called Thomas Tornow's opulent office in downtown Whitefish, Montana. Following a hasty, "My name is..." I blurted out, "How in the world did you get a copy of *Tornow* in Montana?" Seemingly of a humorous temperament, the attorney chuckled before answering, "Let me tell you the funny story of how that happened."

Even if his legal timeclock had been ticking off dollars for the minutes, I would have willingly paid. Tom Tornow's brother . . . now pay attention to this . . . *John* Tornow, was a physician from San Francisco who was relocating to the Puget Sound country. I could hear the undertones of his sniggering as he related the story. "John was in a bookstore at the Seattle airport when he spotted a bookcover with his own name on a tombstone. Right there on the cover of this book, the stone proclaimed his death on April 16, 1913. Needless to say, he was rather distraught. Tornow is not a real common name for coincidences to occur." The lawyer continued, "He bought two copies and sent one to me. We enjoyed your book very much."

"Have you determined if there is any relationship with the Matlock Tornows?" I asked.

"We think not," he replied. "It must have been a different family tree in a different forest."

When I related all this to Al, he laughed, "Ain't that a corker?" slapping his knee with a hearty howl.

A few months later I came into contact with Dr. John Tornow, inviting him and his wife to the 1998 Matlock Old Timer's Fair in May. We enjoyed talking Tornow-lore and introducing the Tornows to interested fair patrons. Our colossal planet can sometimes become miniaturized to nothing more than Mr. Roger's neighborhood.

Lesson # 218. Some perceived threats can become delightful windfalls.

Through the balance of 1997 the book continued moving quickly off retailer's shelves. Up front, on the boiler-plate page, I had listed my address plus, "Copies of this book may be obtained by sending $16.00, including sales tax, p & h, to..." So we sold some books via direct mail.

At a few accounts, Al and I couldn't keep ahead of sales. I established one sales territory of six or eight small convenience stores, gas stations and restaurants adjacent to a rural highway. The retailers were scattered beside the twenty-mile long road which was an hour's drive from home. We left account ABC at three o'clock one afternoon, heading for the home barn. Arriving, Kit said, "Mrs. So and So at ABC called, said she's out of books and needs more."

"We left her five books about an hour ago," I replied, thinking there had to be some mistake.

"Yes," Kit said, "she mentioned you'd just been there, but she had customers waiting and they bought all you'd left."

I mailed her five more. In situations like that, I found U.S. mail, book rate, was the best means of quick and inexpensive delivery. Book rate meant *just* books; no letters; notes; or writing. At the time, one book cost $1.24 to mail (now $1.13), getting progressively less expensive for more books. I often mailed packages of five books for $2.75, less than the wear and tear would be on Cherokee to drive there—much less.

144

Dick Moulton serviced a quaint restaurant in the small town of Elma, Washington, by the catchy name of "Rusty Tractor."

"You'd be surprised how many books they sell from that little rack of mine that sits on the back-bar in the counter section. Last week alone they sold ten copies of *Tornow,*" Dick said.

"In that little place?" I questioned.

"Yep, their customers must read a lot. Let's do a book signing and see what happens."

"In that little place?" I reiterated.

Al and I started off the morning of September 5th at a signing at the Rusty Tractor. We headquartered on a small table near the cafe's front door. With only minimal in-restaurant pre-signs we sold a dozen books to locals who dropped by for breakfast, or coffee, or just to chat and buy a book. It was unbelievable. Whenever I was in the area, I dropped in for coffee, and to check their book inventory. If Dick hadn't stopped within the previous week, chances are they needed books which I supplied from my car-inventory.

* * *

In October, 1997, our local library sponsored an author's event that brought together more than 100 Western Washington writers where we had an opportunity to meet the public and sell our books. I felt honored to be in such celebrated company, plus I sold ten books.

Two months after receiving 2,000 books from Gorham, I did a quick inventory check.

"I can't believe it, but there's only 200 books in my inventory," I told Kit one October morning.

"At that rate, we won't make it to Christmas."

"You'd better re-order," Kit suggested.

"It will be a minimum of 1,000 for a good price," I said. "Kurt will probably do 1,000 at about the same price per book as the original 2,000. He has all the plates and mats or whatever he uses left, so he can do a reprint for less. But 1,000 books on top of the 2,000 that will be out there, sure sounds like a lot," I told Kit. "Hope we can sell them."

On December 3, 1977 Al and I picked up 1,000 books, the second printing from Gorham's, barely in time for several Christmas gift-giving signing events we had scheduled. Late 1997 also provided additional publicity through two radio interviews on local Tacoma stations, including one of my favorites, Dorothy Wilhelm.

I was also invited to talk about the life of John Tornow at a Hoquiam High School assembly of 120 freshmen and sophomore students. I congratulated them for being a quiet, attentive and responsive audience, asking many thought-provoking questions. Teachers and students bought eight books that morning. Most youngsters seemed quite interested in the Tornow story. I enjoyed putting on a 45-minute program for these young Hoquiam Grizzlies and reaching into a new marketing area.

* * *

Tallying sales in November, 1997, I couldn't believe some of the records we'd established. Dick Moulton had distributed 656 *Tornow*; Brady Food Mart, a small country store, had sold 58; Billie Howard at the Shelton Historical Museum had taken 56 copies. That was all in less than three months. I feared that at some point we might hit a saturation level.

But, there was also an occasional downside to our success story. I had approached a local supermarket about a signing which we scheduled on December 13th. The store was in a group advertising program and I doubted they could publicize a signing in the ad for just one individual store.

"If you will get the copy and a picture to me at least three weeks prior, we can get it in the ad," the manager said.

I delivered the ad copy a month before the signing, asking him, "Is there any other means of publicity?"

"Oh, yes, I'll put it on our reader board a few days before the scheduled date. We can make it a real community affair. I'll have the bakery bake us a large cake, and we'll serve cake and coffee," he concluded.

I began to feel comfortable that we could put together a successful signing although I still doubted his ability to insert the event into his cooperative advertising program.

The grocery ad broke on Wednesday prior to the Saturday session—no mention of the book signing. On Thursday prior, no P.R. on the reader board so I reminded the manager who said, "We'll put it up this afternoon."

All prepared for the three-hour event, I arrived twenty-minutes early. I'd had no newspaper mention; still nothing on the reader board; no cake and coffee. I was tempted to turn around and go home. "Where's the manager?" I asked.

"Today's his day off," the clerk said. I was beginning to think this guy's elevator didn't go up to the first floor.

I suffered through a most boring three hours—selling a grand total of two books.

Lesson #219. Don't count signings until they're advertised.

Book sales were forgotten during January, 1998 as Kit and I "snowbirded" to Palm Springs. While there, I visited an import store where I stumbled across a white-wire plate stand. It was constructed to display a decorative plate upright. I bought one; it only cost two bucks. Instead of a plate, I envisioned displaying a *Tornow* book in it, then locating it on a retailer's counter near the checkstand. Only problem, it would only hold one book, two if I squeezed them.

Returning home in February, while wandering through a Dollar store, I spotted a rack similar to a countertop dish drainer, made from the same stuff as the plate holder.

Before I say more, I want to state at this point that I believe the discovery of this simple, dumb dish drainer was the primary key to our continuing success with *Tornow*. In effect, it became our "secret weapon." I picked up the dish drainer, turned it over and over,

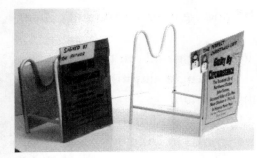

These simple little wire racks were our "secret weapon." From a one-dollar dish drainer, four hacksaw cuts produced two racks. The larger rack holds nine books, the smaller rack accomodates five.

These racks of books were placed on high-volume retailer counters, and sold a significant number of the 5,000 plus books sold. Stores endorsed the racks because they occupied minimal space, made the book highly visible, and when placed near cashier checkouts, provided book security.

trying to envision a book display rack. I bought one for only a buck, as is everything at the Dollar store.

I continued studying the wire dish drainer at home and told Kit, "There's something important here if only I can figure it out." In haste I grabbed my hacksaw and began sawing up sections of the drainer. Catastrophe! Thanks to my impatience, that dish drainer had flat died right there on my work bench. I'd severed its main arteries, hacked off its limbs, with nothing to show for the operation except a nondescript pile of white-wire pieces. But then, I saw my mistake. I'd amputated in the wrong places.

This author, cum engineer, cum surgeon, could hardly wait to get back to the Dollar store to buy another dish drainer. What the heck, I thought, only a buck. Let's buy two so we'll have a spare this time. Knowing exactly what to do, I made just four cuts. Perfect! The small rack I'd produced had a capacity of five books standing upright. The second rack, from the same drainer, held nine books, same position.

Major contributors to the *Tornow* success, the racks had several attributes. Almost all retailers accepted them because they occupied minimal counter space, no more than the equivalent number of books would require *without* a rack. The books were displayed upright so it was an attention-grabber. Two vertical wires on front formed a frame for attaching a 4x6-inch advertising sign. Producing two racks from a one-dollar drainer had provided an inexpensive display rack. At fifty-cents each, it wouldn't break the bank if we occasionally lost a couple of racks. What a screamer!

One March morning as I picked up Al to check a territory where I had placed books, I noticed he was in a pensive mood.

"I've been thinking," Al said, "here I am spending all day with you checking out customers, when I could be doing this for myself."

"Do you want to set up an apple box on the corner and start selling books?" I facetiously inquired.

"No, no, and don't misunderstand me," he continued, "I enjoy tagging along with you, but I'm a retired salesman and should be out selling, not as a retailer, but as a distributor."

"Makes sense to me," I replied, "what do you have in mind?"

"If I become a distributor, would you sell books to me at wholesale and allow me to pay you when the retailers pay me?" Al asked.

Pointing Cherokee across the Tacoma Narrows Bridge on that frosty winter morning, I thought about Al's question.

"As long as you assume responsibility for all books you take, I have no problem with what you're proposing. In fact, I'd welcome it, more sales mean better profits. I don't necessarily care *when* I'm paid, as long as it happens within a reasonable length of time.

We discussed territories. "It's important that you don't spill over into any areas already supplied by me, Moulton, or customers serviced by the Seattle distributors."

"I'm thinking about Centralia, Chehalis, Olympia, maybe smaller accounts in Tacoma, even north toward Seattle," Al said.

I showed Al my new fifty-cent rack, even gave him a few with the small cardstock signs taped on front. Within a few days, Al and I cleaned out the nearby Dollar stores of the dish drainers.

As I bought ten one day, the cashier asked, "What in the world are you going to do with ten dish drainers?"

"Shh," I whispered, "don't tell anyone but these racks help us sell books." I savored the bewildered look on her face. "Books?" she questioned in disbelief, screwing up her mouth like a wrinkled prune.

Al was a helluva salesman. He began pounding the pavement, selling to supermarkets, restaurants, convenience stores, even florists and barbershops. The little white racks displaying the *Tornow* books began popping up all over Western Washington. Al developed over 100 new retail accounts. I estimated we had a grand total counting all distributors of more than 300 outlets. I also wore out three hacksaw blades.

"I placed five books at the barber who cuts my hair each month," he told me one day.

"*Tornow* books in a barbershop!" I exclaimed. "They won't sell."

The first week, I was right; second week they sold out. After that, sales were steady, but in 6 to 8 weeks he hit the saturation point, because the customers were mainly "regulars." The book pipeline overflowed.

"I hope you don't mind," Al said one day. "I sold a book to 'our' dentist, and last week I sold one to 'our' doctor." By coincidence, Al and I both had the same dentist and same cardiologist. I was too reserved to hustle professionals whom I saw on a regular schedule. Not Al! He didn't care who it was. He would sell the devil himself as long as the greenbacks were the right color.

Towards the end of March, Al's sales, plus the other distributors, plus the ongoing readings and signings depleted our book inventory once again. It was unbelievable! We'd sold almost 3,000 books in less than eight months. I became somewhat concerned that, as we took on new retail outlets, our unsold inventory in each one of those 150, or so, little racks was going to begin piling up. Al and I discussed this potential hazard. He opined, "We should be o.k. as long as we don't pile on excess new inventory on top of existing dead stock."

"Yes, I agree, and if records indicate that some accounts aren't moving any books, let's pull them out and place them where they *are* selling," I suggested.

As soon as Al identified an account with a good book-selling track record, we scheduled a signing session. As he moved into a new territory, I contacted the area newspaper and sold them on the idea of running a John Tornow feature article.

It was late March when Kurt Gorham received my order for the third edition. With a feigned serious tone he asked, "What are you guys doing with all those books, giving them away on the street corners?"

"Have you looked around your own little town?" Al asked.

"Yes, I've seen a few familiar-looking books around town," he replied.

In the tiny community of Rochester, we had six outlets, including the Indian gambling casino a few miles up the road.

Retiring from a grocery career, Al had many friends in the supermarkets. He enlisted one such friend across the freeway from the Olympia Brewery. It became another outlet where Al had a difficult time maintaining the *Tornow* book inventory. As a last resort, he put four racks in the store, one on every second checkstand. With a well-written feature article in the *Daily Olympian,* mentioning our scheduled signings in the area, we enjoyed tremendous sales. Two Olympia-area supermarkets sold over 100 books each in just six months.

As our total number of signing sessions climbed towards the century mark, we began to see a trend which retail grocery execs are probably aware of, but which should be reemphasized. Stores with the best sales records with us were those where managers and assistants spent a lot of time in the checkstand areas, visiting and joking with customers, asking and answering questions, even bagging groceries when the store was busy, and offering to carry out parcels.

"Look at this one," Al would whisper as we walked in, "dead as flies in a freezer."

"Could we please talk with the manager?" I asked.

"He's upstairs," the cashier grumbled.

No pizazz, no vibrancy and hardly any courtesy usually spelled no customers.

On the other hand, we walked into Al's account that had sold more than a hundred *Tornows*. It was a Thursday, not necessarily the busiest shopping day, but all ten checkstands were clanging. Manager Earl was bagging groceries for a lady when he spotted Al and me coming through the double-doors. "Look who's here," he yelled across the lobby, "I knew we should have locked those doors." Hearing this, smiling customers looked up, knowing Earl was ribbing a just-arrived victim. He only took time for a couple of quick handshakes.

Big Jim, the assistant, was checking on number four. I'd never seen him without an ear-to-ear grin; today was no different. "Hi, guys, come in and join the circus," he chuckled.

The customers loved it, and the managers were having fun, too.

While we're still here in Olympia, the state capitol, I have another incident to share. Early summer of 1998, on a Saturday afternoon, I had scheduled a book signing at Barnes & Noble. Things were moving along o.k. We'd sold 6-8 books when I looked up, recognizing three customers hurrying in the front door. I'll be darned, I thought to myself, it's Washington's Governor, Gary Locke, his wife, Mona Lee, and their daughter, Emily. They were obviously trying to be inconspicuous. The Gov was dressed in jeans and short-sleeves. I wanted to walk up and greet them, but then thought better of it. No, they don't want to be recognized, so I won't spoil it for them.

As quickly as they'd entered, they paid for a small purchase

STATE OF WASHINGTON
OFFICE OF THE GOVERNOR

P.O. Box 40002 • Olympia, Washington 98504-0002 • (360) 753-6780 • FAX (360) 753-4110 • TTY/TDD (360) 753-6466

June 19, 1998

Ron Fowler
44 Leschi Drive
Steilacoom, WA 98388

Dear Ron:

Thank you very much for forwarding to me an autographed copy of your book, *Guilty by Circumstance*. I appreciated hearing from you.

Education is my top priority as governor, and clearly the key to education is reading. I am always amazed at the wide variety of reading material available today. Your work on the life of outlaw John Tornow sounds quite intriguing and I look forward to learning more about him and his role in the history of the great Northwest.

Again, thank you for your thoughtful gift, and be sure to say hi the next time you see me in a bookstore!

Sincerely,

Gary Locke
Governor

Washington's Governor Gary Locke responded to a letter and copy of book, Guilty By Circumstance, sent to him by the author. Education, and the history of the Northwest are of high interest to Governor Locke.

and zipped out the door without recognition. The next day I wrote them a brief letter acknowledging I had seen them while signing books. I enclosed the letter with a gratis copy of *Tornow*, and mailed it to the governor.

Within a week, or two, I received a "thank you" letter from Governor Locke for the book, along with his invitation, "...be sure to say hi next time you see me in a bookstore."

What a great guy! I think I'll vote for him in the next election, even though he is a Democrat.

✳

Chapter 12

There are several Indian gambling casinos in the general area of the state where we sold books. Al calculated the casino gift shops would be a logical place to sell books—logical to Al, at least.

Permission to solicit the casinos and also a trading post on the reservation came through an off-site administrative office. That was no problem for agent Al. I think he may have softened the chief procurement officer by claiming to be a certified member of the U.S. Polack clan.

Book sales at the two side-by-side locations were a whopping success, but on a back and forth basis. One trip, the casino would sell out, while the market sales were flat. Next trip, the opposite prevailed. However, between the two customers they accounted for almost a hundred books in six months. We weren't hesitant to return some of our profits to the Indian Tribe by way of the casino, often shedding doubt on who actually collected the most dollars. Their entertainment provided at the tables was well worth the expenditures.

Early in Al's book-selling career, he tackled one of the leviathan supermarket chains and succeeded in placing *Tornow* in a half-dozen of their Puget Sound area stores, Olympia to Seattle. Masterful marketing by the officers of this firm had been responsible for their success and large slice of market share enjoyed by these stores. These people knew how to merchandise and promote, including our books.

From barbers, to doctors, to corporate board executives, the big and the little, Al took 'em all on with both feet in the door.

We held signing sessions at five of the six nearby locations of the successful supermarket chain—the best ones we did twice.

They gave our little white racks space near their busiest checkstands and it wasn't unusual for them to sell out a rack of ten books over a busy weekend.

Al was mostly dealing with general merchandise clerks in those stores. All of them were extremely astute and quite capable. I tagged along on the day he delivered books to the more distant store, arranging inventory prior to establishing a booksigning.

"I'd like to put in two wire racks, each holding ten books, on this checkstand display board," Al suggested to the merchandiser.

"How many books in a full case?" she asked.

"Fifty-two," Al gulped, his eyes wide open in anticipation.

"Use the entire display area, bring in a full case," she directed. "Mass merchandising sells, you know."

Walking out to the car for books, Al said, tongue-in-cheek, "That's what I've always told you, Ron, big displays sell books, ya gotta think big!"

In that same little town near Seattle, we also placed five books in a downtown independent bookstore.

"We'd better contact the local weekly newspaper and try to sell them on a *Tornow* feature story to tie-in with the signing," I suggested. "We'll need to have a dynamite promotion to sell all those 52 books you talked her into taking. "The paper's associate editor interviewed us first and, fortunately, was a history enthusiast.

"I like your material and the story about the outlaw," he said, "we should be able to develop a feature and pictures to coincide with your supermarket signing." Wonderful, I thought to myself, breathing a sigh of relief over the 52 books.

"But you'll need the editor's approval." This could shoot us down, I thought.

The editor was not a history fan—he was a, "Is it local?" disciple.

Alloting me a few minutes of his time, he asked, "Are you a local author, or is it a local story?"

"Afraid not."

"We could only support a story like this if the author was from around here," he said.

I mentally calculated cobwebs forming on all 52 of the books in the supermarket. "But, the two retailers who are selling my books are local," I pleaded.

"Yes, but not generating much advertising revenue," he responded. "Do you want to buy an ad to promote your book?"

"What is your rate per column inch?" I inquired. "There's not much profit in writing and selling books."

With the rate he quoted, I calculated if we sold all 52 books, we'd break even. Pete's favorite line, "...I sure hope to break even on this deal..." came to mind.

I told the editor, "Let me think about this and if at all possible I'll write-up a small ad and mail it to you with my check."

"That will be o.k. I guess we'll have space to run a story that week and support your signing," he said. I feared the story might be contingent on buying an ad.

Later, at home, I gave considerable thought to our "Catch 22" position in that town. Running a small 2x4-inch ad amounted to over a hundred-dollars at the rate we'd been given.

"Can't afford it," I told Al, "I'd rather have the books back."

I wrote the editor a polite letter, again mentioning the lack of profitability. I enclosed a check for fifty-dollars, plus wording for a 2x4-inch ad, and ended my letter, "Please run whatever size ad this check will buy."

"You'll probably get a two-liner in the classifieds," Al said facetiously.

Three weeks later, arriving at the town for the signing session, we could hardly wait to buy a paper to see how much publicity we'd received. The associate editor had done a splendid job of running a feature article on *Tornow* and the signing. Last but not least, at the bottom of the page was my 2x4-inch ad, just as I'd written it. To date, it was the only time I paid for newspaper advertising.

Lesson #220. Expect the good things, plan for all others.

Even with the publicity, we didn't set any new international sales records at the supermarket. I sold about twenty books, but we were rather far afield from John Tornow country. Most of the remaining books on the supermarket display sold out during the next few weeks. The merchandiser had clipped the newspaper story, laminated it in plastic, and displayed the article near the book display.

In contrast, indicative of the lack of know-how by some business people, the downtown bookstore didn't sell one book.

"Didn't the write-up in the newspaper move out any of my books?" I asked the owner.

"What write-up?" he asked.

We picked up the five books a few weeks later, no sale, no charge.

"If that owner was on the ball, he would have cut out the article and displayed the books right up front like the market merchandiser did," Al lamented.

I felt bad that the store had failed to capitalize on the Tornow newspaper publicity—especially my 'bargain' ad.

Two of the same regional chain's supermarkets were located in the Olympia-area where the daily newspaper had splashed with an excellent feature article on John Tornow and our book signings. We couldn't ride in on the market's advertising coat-tails, again because of multiple stores in the same ad.

"Why don't you consider bag-stuffers?" one of the store's merchandisers suggested. "We sometimes have the baggers at the checkstands insert stuffers for several days prior to an event."

"That might be a good idea," I replied, "how many stuffers would we have to print?"

"Well, she said, we've got ten checkstands, and we average around 6,000 customers a day."

"Sufferin' succotash!" I screamed. "You're talking big bucks. Could we try maybe just a thousand."

"Sure, we could spread them out over several days prior to the signing. I'll tell the baggers to ration them carefully," she grinned, but only with her eyes.

"Maybe they could just put the stuffers into grocery bags of people who read books," Al kidded her.

A local office supply store ran a special promotion of $18.00 for a thousand, 8½x11-inch colored paper copies. Thinking we could double our output to two-thousand if we printed two stuffers on each sheet, then cut them in half, I developed the copy. It began, "You are cordially invited to a special book signing at_____on for Ron Fowler's historical NW book, *Guilty By Circumstance*, the John Tornow story."

We paid a couple bucks to have them whacked in half on a mechanical paper-cutter. Scissors didn't seem like a viable option considering the cost. Al and I split the expense.

We delivered the 2,000 bag-stuffers to the store and their personnel distributed them on the Friday-Saturday preceding our in-store signing. Oh yes, it was the second signing we'd had at that market. We didn't arrive at a solid conclusion about the bag-stuffers. I sold a considerable number of books, not as many as the earlier signing, but that was to be expected.

Like Al theorized, "We really don't know if we got our twenty-bucks worth, or not."

While we're talking printed P.R. material, I did a mailer prior to my local book signings. Kinko's had an attractive, full-sheet stationery page with a border of flora and fauna across the top and down one edge, blank in the middle and right edge for copy. I worked up a "personal invitation" message similar to the bag-stuffer, and listed times and places for several upcoming signings/readings. This was mailed to all of our close neighbors, friends, and relatives in the vicinity of the sessions. Not an "arm-twister," but just—come if you can.

I think many customers attended our book signings just to have somebody to talk to—or more aptly phrased—someone who would listen to them. Seems like they always want to bend my ear at the same time someone wanted me to personalize a book.

There was a fellow like that in Chehalis, said he was a semi-retired fireman. Before the day was over I'd wished he'd had a fire somewhere to put out. I couldn't get away from him. He talked to me continuously, his jaw clicking a mile a minute. He even rudely interrupted me when I tried to talk with a legitimate customer. Be aware such problem-people exist.

"Maybe his wife is deaf and he can't talk to her," Al suggested.

"I think he's certifiable," I replied.

We developed a plan that fell flat as a railroad-squashed penny. I told Al, "Please have the store page me on the intercom for a telephone call. Maybe then I can just walk away from him."

Returning from the fictitious phone call, I ambled back to the signing table. Sure enough, there he sat by himself, waiting for me. Soon as I sat down he started talking again about his Aunt Myrtle on his mother's side who… Maybe if I turned in a false fire alarm that would get rid of him. And he didn't even buy a book! My, oh my, this business was more fun than a playground.

There is a scenic loop Highway 101 that goes around Washington's Olympic Peninsula, a total drive of about 400-miles.

The road passes through magnificent ocean-mountain-forest country and is a popular summer tourist route. There are a dozen small to medium size towns and resorts along the scenic byway.

I felt certain we could sell *Tornow* books through retail outlets on the loop highway. In early May, 1998 I loaded the car (gave

Cherokee a rest) with several boxes of books, advertising material, consignment forms, Kit, and an overnight bag.

Our prospecting began at restaurants, convenience stores, and trailer parks along the crooked road tracing the western shores of placid Hood Canal. We canvassed the waterfront!

Utilizing the consignment concept of no pay until sold, few retailers turned me down. When we pulled into a motel in Port Angeles the first evening, I had "sold" 20 customers, placing 75 books. The second day I contacted 16 customers before arriving at Aberdeen-Hoquiam, Dick Moulton's territory and off-limits to me. In the two days we drove over 400-miles, placed 119 books with 36 customers, turned down by only two retailers. I knew the test wouldn't be validated until the return junket.

Due to the geographic location and added expenses of the jaunt, I felt justified in charging an extra dollar for the book, $8.00 for a $13.95 retail provided a 43% profit for the retailer with no investment and unlimited return privilege.

May through September is the primary tourist season around the loop and we split it up into four trips, the last one was in early October when I picked up all books and made a final collection. We didn't stay overnight on that trip, driving straight thru, a total of almost 14-hours.

Highway 101 passes through one tidy little town where we had an unusual experience. There are no chain bookstores on the scenic circle until returning to the larger towns. There were two independent bookstores in the small town and both agreed to stock the *Tornow* book. One shop, operated by a rather unorthodox type of individual, asked if I could do a booksigning on our next trip around the loop highway.

"Sure, we can work one in, maybe a couple of hours on a Friday afternoon," I told the proprietor. "Can you request a feature article in your local newspaper?"

"I don't know about that, the editor is kind of different and hard to do business with."

Was this the kettle calling the pot black? I thought to myself.

I told the owner that I would mail a couple of publicity signs to display in the store prior to the signing. "Also, I'll drop off a press release at the newspaper and see if we can drum up some publicity," I said.

The place just didn't feel right to me, especially having a signing with minimal chances of newspaper publicity. Later, I told Kit, "The population here must be a few thousand, many retirees, but that bookstore didn't have a single customer the entire time I was in there, and the owner seems to be a little bit strange."

A month later we scheduled our second trip around the loop. Sales had been just fair at the first batch of retailers we called on. They reported the tourist season wasn't yet in full swing. I collected for a few, consigned additional copies, hurried to meet my scheduled signing appointment—with a certain trepidation. There had been no newspaper publicity, still no customers in the store, although the signs I'd mailed were displayed. The owner was just as different as when we made our earlier trip.

During the first hour of the signing session two customers meandered through the bright, clean, well-stocked little shop.

They ignored me like I was a pitch-blister on a fir tree. Finally, on that warm summer afternoon, a man dressed in Levis came in and sauntered over to my table.

"Can I interest you in a copy of my Northwest outlaw book?" I asked cheerfully.

"Already got one," he replied, "just brought it in for you to sign."

This surprised me because I'd tried to sign every book delivered to retailers with my favorite, slash-printed signature.

Beyond that, I personalized them further at our signings with salutations such as, "To Hortense, have a good Tornow read," etc. Looking at his book's title page I found the copy was signed like all others. Holding it up for him to see, I said, "It's signed right here."

"That ain't no signature," he replied.

"It's the way I sign all my books."

"I don't care none about that, I want a written signature," he said.

For just a fleeting moment I wanted to arch my back and refuse to give that guy something I hadn't given on 5,000 other copies of the book. Then I remembered the golden rule that all people in business should tatoo across their forehead, "The customer is always right."

"O.K.," I relented, "I'll sign it in longhand but you might not be able to read it, my scribbling is not the best."

After that, we became good buddies. He told me several wild stories about all the trees he'd sawed down, and a few other unbelievable tales. I'd had a few pieces of free literature on the table and he scooped up every one on his way out the door.

During four months I sold a total of *one* book in that little town, but from another bookstore.

In contrast, the next town down the road, of about the same population, took to *Tornow* like a penguin takes to ice cubes. I had five outlets in the town, including the "Hungry Bear Cafe," located a few miles out in the timber from city center. During that summer, we sold well over a hundred books in the tiny community.

There was a bookstore on the main drag operated by a friendly young couple. They were eager to schedule a book-signing with me.

"Will the local newspaper run a story about *Tornow*?" I asked with some amount of reservation.

"Sure," the owners replied, "leave us the information and we'll schedule an article with the editor. He's very supportive of local business. Leave some pictures, too, he'll run them with the story. And don't forget to mail us a couple of your personalized signing announcement signs. We'll display them soon as they arrive."

The signing event at the bookstore on our next trip through was awesome for a small town. We sold about 20 books and had the good fortune to meet and chat with many local residents, salt-of-the-earth type people, rural Americana that can be discovered almost everywhere across our great country.

Why? Why the difference? Two very similar towns but with such dissimilar results. Was it because of the newspaper? A supportive editor in one town and a nonparticipant in the other? I wrote a letter of thanks to the supportive editor.

We could never understand the disparity, just explained it away with, "That's the book business."

Lesson #221. Don't question the unquestionable.

On this same loop route, I had consigned five books to a small convenience store operator with a limited command of English. He was a bit reluctant, but opted to take on the books, directing me to display them with his greeting cards in the back of the store. I knew that was not a highly productive location for them.

On my first return trip, he hadn't sold one book. Determined to get my wire rack displayed near the front counter, or pull the books out if I was not allowed to move them, I explained to the operator that high-profit merchandise warranted top billing in his store. I was not sure he understood my pitch but he agreed to move the rack up front.

Next jaunt through the territory, I spotted my white rack in the same place on the counter where I'd left it. Empty.

"Where's the books?" I asked.

"All sold," he replied.

"Want more?"

"Sure, bring five more," he said.

"O.K., I'll collect for five and consign another five," I told the operator. That day he learned a few merchandising pointers.

Total sales for the four trips around the loop were close to 300 books, not enough to justify the expenses, but Kit and I enjoyed the welcome break from our home-bound routine. It had been a good ride!

While on the subject of customers without a good understanding of English, enter one of Al's retailers, not long in our country, a convenience store operator. I was with Al when he gave this unfortunate immigrant the sales pitch.

"We leave the books on consignment, you don't have to pay for them up front, just sign the receipt and we leave, pay later," Al tried to explain. In retrospect, he should have gone into more detail, perhaps offered a deeper explanation.

We went back to the store in a couple of weeks. The rack was empty. "Where books?" Al asked.

Beaming a wide, toothed grin, the owner replied, "All gone, books all gone. You got more?"

I could just imagine the fellow was thinking that America was the greatest land he'd ever seen—maybe a little bit crazy and difficult to understand, but real champion.

"Sure," Al replied. "I'll collect from you for the five you've sold and leave five more."

"Collect?" the bewildered operator repeated, "You mean money?"

"That was our deal, no pay until sold," Al said.

"But you say books no charge. How you say...consignment? We no sell books, we give away to good customers like you tell us."

Al and I looked at each other and then we both realized what had happened. The operator thought "consignment" was just another American word for "free." Al reluctantly collected for the five books by showing the operator the consignment form he had signed. The owner decided he didn't want any more *Tornow* books, probably thought Al was a bigger crook than the Northwest outlaw was.

Small stores weren't the only people doing strange things in our literary livelihoods. Some of our distributors also shared that distinction. One of them had a bothersome habit of sending me small quantities of my book via an overnight freight handler.

Each time it happened, I'd jump on the phone, "Why did you return four copies of my book? Are you discontinuing it from your inventory?"

"No, I don't really know why that happened," the buyer replied.

After the third time, I finally solved the mystery. Whenever a retailer returned books they were set aside in a special section rather than returning them to inventory.

The warehouse people had been given instructions to return items in that section to the author/publisher. Turning a deaf ear to my pleading, I could never get this policy rescinded. They might even buy a full case of books from me on the same day they returned three or four quite saleable copies.

The same distributor had quite a frugal payment system to authors/publishers. Yet, one day they sent me a check for $1300.00 to which I was not entitled. They seemed reluctant to have me return the check because their system had no provision or procedure for processing returned funds. I think the clerks would have preferred I keep the overpayment and just forget about the whole thing. But, I didn't.

Our book distributors didn't have a monopoly on unusual practices. Al and I went into one of my large retail bookstores one day to check their inventory. I had scheduled a signing with them, but it was about a month away.

Checking their computer, the clerk said, "Oh dear, we are out of your book but we show 25 on order."

"When will they arrive?" I asked, "you don't have a single *Tornow* book on the shelf."

"Talk with our assistant in back," she suggested, "I know customers have been asking for your book. Maybe they have arrived and are in the backroom."

Finding said assistant, she also queried the computer, "For some reason, I think those 25 might already be here. Let me look," she said.

In single file the three of us traipsed up to the front of the store. "Yes," she reported, "here they are in the hold section."

"Why are you holding them while turning away customers?" I asked.

"Well, let's see. Oh, I know, you have a signing session scheduled, don't you?" she inquired.

"Yes, but it's a month away. How long does it take for you to receive books after they're ordered?"

"Oh, just a day or two," she said.

"Then why don't you put some of these on the shelf for immediate sale and reorder for the signing?"

"That would be against our policy," she explained with the same face.

I felt like screaming to break the frustration. But it probably wouldn't do any good. After a half-hour of pleading, involving the manager, trying to explain it was just common sense, and to hell with policy, they very reluctantly placed six copies on the shelf for customers to buy. I'm sure the manager and clerks involved thought they were putting their jobs in extreme jeopardy.

Those were just a few of the crazy events we experienced as we began to learn about the book business. Like the sign I spotted in a small bookstore tucked away on a dead-end street.

It said: "If you cannot read English, the foreign language section is located in aisle seven."

I suppose the sign was posted for humor. Or was it?

Write a Newsy

Before sallying forth on an authorship career, you may want to test your skills by composing one of the typical holiday "newsletters" often found tucked into Christmas cards. Although considerably short of "typical," here's our rendition. We are beginning to think about compiling a annual holiday newsletter chronicling all the family happenings from the past year. We cannot take credit for this idea. Many of our friends and relatives generate this type of newsy letter each holiday.

As you read between the lines, you'll understand the considerable enjoyment we derive from each missive.

* * *

This year will be a most memorable time for us and we plan a spectacular party in honor of our son, Jimmy, who will be released from prison after serving only nineteen years of his twenty-year sentence for armed robbery. Such a wonderful boy!

He is really the joy of our life. But, just imagine, they knocked off a whole year, 365 days, due to his extremely good behavior. Of course, we felt he was unjustly accused in the first place. Bless his heart, he tried in vain to explain to the authorities that his Glock 19 fired by mistake during the holdup and he had absolutely no intention of hurting those seventeen bystanders from the church group.

We're keeping our fingers crossed that the oldest daughter, the love of our life, Melody Ann, will complete her drug treatment program in time to join the celebration for her brother's release.

Such a wonderful girl. We're assuming the state will not press charges against her for possession with intent to sell. We testified earlier that she could not possibly have known those ten kilos were in the trunk of her Lamborghini. Someone had to put them in her car by mistake. The police never would have found those drugs if she hadn't plowed into the minister's car at approximately 100 m.p.h. Poor child. She is just the victim of unusual circumstances.

You'll be thrilled to hear that earlier this year we celebrated the marriage of my sixty-nine year-old aunt to her eighty-seven year-old childhood sweetheart. We only discuss it within the family as Auntie was pregnant at the time of the wedding ceremony. Such an impetuous couple! She has always supplied the moral fiber that represents the high level of righteousness within our family. We wish the newlyweds a long and happy life together as they honeymoon at Disneyland.

I know you're all anxious to hear how our new transportation business is going. Well, fret no more. With sixteen trucks on the road every night, business is booming. We did experience a minor setback when the border authorities confiscated one of our rigs returning with a load from Canada.

It was the first time we'd ever heard it was illegal to bring whiskey across the border. They probably wouldn't have bothered the truck if it hadn't been overloaded by 11½ tons, and the driver had passed his sobriety test. Picky-picky.

Boopy, our lovable, eighty-nine pound Pit Bull lap dog has suffered more than her share of ailments this year. Poor thing. It all began with her indigestion after she ate the mailman's leather bag. We're just a bit concerned because he's threatening to sue as soon as he's released from intensive care, and can walk without crutches. If that's not bad enough, Boopy's tongue is constantly sticking to the roof of her mouth from the glue that was on the stamps and envelopes.

We had a marvelous vacation trip to Central America this year despite being detained for two weeks by the guerilla rebels, and held captive in that nasty, damp jungle cave. We told them there was no way our government would pay twenty million dollars for our release. I think they had us confused with another American couple, the Rockefellers.

I could go on and on, including the story about how I lost my nicest pair of brown loafers that I was wearing when the mowing machine amputated both of my feet. The doctor believes I have made a miraculous recovery and estimates I'll become accustomed to my prosthesis in just a few short years. I loved those shoes!

Oh yes, we want to reassure everyone the fire was not nearly as devastating as first reported. You may recall, our cat, Muffy, unfortunately knocked over a kerosene lamp we were using after the utility company turned off our power following the quarter-million dollar remodeling job on our home. We'll probably have to take the insurance company to court because they say this kind of a cat-astrophe is not a covered peril in our policy, notwithstanding the fact it expired three months before the fire. Why should that make any difference?

After the house burned to the ground, the humane society sent out a team of five experts to tranquilize and take Muffy to a zoo. We'd never heard it was against the law to keep spotted African leopards as house pets. We'll miss that lovable little kitty.

You'll hear more of these family happenings in our next holiday newsletter. It will include details of our planned tenting vacation to Indonesia's Komodo Island where we plan to catch and bring home some of those adorable little monitor lizards.

Epilogue

As we wrote "Finis-30" to the last books of the last printing of *Tornow*, Al and I were astonished by one aspect of our book-selling experience. Neither of us lost one penny—one book—one bum check, as a result of peddling almost 6,000 copies of two books to retailers, distributors, booklovers, bookworms, even a few suspicious-looking characters. Without checking references, bank balances, or past rap sheets of potential customers, we distributed thousands of books on consignment, on blind faith. We weren't bushwhacked once.

"Pay nothing up front, we'll collect after you sell them," was our happy-go-lucky tune to shop owners as they signed the consignment form. Dozens of people wrote checks for individual book purchases, as well as sizeable store quantities. None came back NSF.

During the year several readers told me, "I want one of your books, but I don't have my checkbook today."

I told them all, "Take a book, here's my card and address. Mail me a check later." Every one of them followed through. Only one customer, a young lady in Elma, needed a reminder. Upon mailing her check, she apologized for her tardiness. Other distributors and retailers find this unblemished collection report quite remarkable. We'd heard stories of shops going out of business, leaving distributors high and dry—no payment—and even worse—no returned inventory. One responsible lady merchant in the tiny community of Malone, Washington, called me as a reminder one day to stop and collect when she realized she would soon be closing her doors. Bless her heart, and all those hundreds of conscientious (and solvent) people whose actions reaffirmed our belief in the trustworthiness of humanity.

One segment of the book business I've failed to mention is the recently-emerged enterprise of Internet online retailing.

In today's electronic era, few business entities remain untouched by our newest online world of computer networking. Kit says, "Anyone not 'cybernated' becomes a discarded flat tire on the crowded Internet highway." Maybe so.

The book industry has been dot-commed extensively, perhaps even transformed into a new beast, by all the latest electronic goings-on. No longer do we need to rush to our friendly library or bookstore to research a pet project. The Net can deliver it, anyway you want it, within seconds, hot off your CRT.

What next? Today we can sell books on the Net; read books on the Net; chat about books on the Net. Will it soon be possible to program our marvelous monoliths to automatically write a bestseller, untouched by human input?

Not wanting to be excluded from a ride on the rapidly ascending starship of electronic distribution, I called Seattle-based Amazon.com in March, 1998, inquiring about getting on board with *Tornow*. A congenial agent responded with an "online submission form," which I completed and returned, along with a gratis copy of the book. No response, no further mailings, no orders, no returned telephone calls, no nothing. An early 1999 news article reported Amazon's 93,000 square-foot warehouse had maxed out at capacity. Maybe they just didn't have any room for *Tornow*.

However, we were not totally ignored by the Internet.

I received an unsolicited book order one rainy afternoon from Barnes&Noble.com which I promptly filled from our dwindling inventory. After all, it's what we do, you know. As of today, with other book vendors climbing aboard, online retailing will undoubtedly become a significant mode of book distribution, if it hasn't already.

As you begin writing and daydreaming about your "Best Seller" awards, here's a few points to remember:

1. Select a subject and title with wide appeal to your "targeted" readers.

2. Dedicate a segment of uninterrupted time on a regular schedule to your writing. Difficult, but you can do it.

3. Share early chapters with someone whose opinion you value for constructive feedback.

4. Be careful not to include any libelous material in your manuscript. When in doubt, check with an attorney as I did.

5. Take time to research publishers/book printers in your local area.

6. Contact retailers who may be willing to schedule signings/readings for your soon-to-be book.

7. Develop marketing logistics and keep an eye out for attractive (and inexpensive) book display holders.

8. Obtain sample forms for consignments and receipts, or, as I did, draft your own. Copy machines are miraculous!

9. Research retail pricing of books similar to yours. Compute retail/wholesale pricing after calculating expenses of printing, distribution, etc. Emphasize selling above cost—important!

10. Enlist your friends to help with local distribution, publicity, marketing, legwork.

11. Plan and strategize publicity which is of utmost importance. Identify a salient point in your book that others can relate to, then make it the centerpiece of your promotion campaign. Investigate all available media outlets; newspapers, tabloids, radio, television, etc.

12. Develop a simple yet thorough means of record-keeping so you will have accurate controls of all your inventory; consigned, sold, returned, paid for, etc.

13. Put off discouragement until tomorrow. Go out and hawk some books.

14. Self-publishing requires money. Don't leave home without it. Good luck. My hat's off to anyone who has the intestinal fortitude (gutsiness) to try it. I did! I just hope some of my experiences will point you in the right (write) direction.

The many techniques we learned about self-publishing and book distribution can best be summarized in two most important, yet simple, words—ingenuity and tenacity. Looking back on our success, especially *Tornow*, it never would have happened if we hadn't emphasized both traits.

Ingenuity is the ability to visualize an efficient, inexpensive, down-home solution to a particular process or problem. The ingenious among us are not necessarily mental masterminds, but usually possess a mega-dose of common sense. That dumb little, fifty-cent wire display rack, and development of media campaigns to publicize the books are two simple examples of ingenuity. Without both, *Tornow* and I would have fallen upon tough times.

To what end do stubborn people remain tenacious? Perhaps receiving 67 "sorry" rejections for *Pete*, my first book, should have convinced me to fold up my tent and study scrimshaw for a hobby. I think tenacity means having confidence in yourself, a belief, or a process—but only up to a point of common sense. Apply virtual reality. Don't emulate the merchant who just kept on a' sellin' 'til the money was all gone. Even a stubborn old bulldog knows better than to climb into the ring with a mountain lion. At some given point, usually determined through common sense, we all need to back down at times.

As I've witnessed and experienced, it seems the most difficult dilemma facing us as authors is the true evaluation of our writings. Will the stuff appeal to the reader—will the public buy it? While a formidable stack of rejections should at least provide a clue to worthiness, by no means are publisher opinions the end of the road, exhibit *Tornow*.

How then do we make the decision whether to be a tenacious bulldog, or Dorothy's lion? If the next plateau is to seek expert advice, please triple-check the credentials of the specialist before depositing coin. I once did otherwise, acquiring a gibbered and disdainful assessment of a particular writing, while contributing several hundreds of dollars to a very worthless cause.

But most importantly—keep writing. Sharpen your skills, study the market, write a winner, either sold to a publisher, or self-published. Don't allow rejection to stifle your determination.

If the literary hand of fate deals you sour grapes, throw them out. Those things taste terrible!

This book was printed by...

(Wouldn't you know it, the printer has to have the last word.)
— Ron